HOW TO GET PERFECT EXPOSURE IN EVERY SITUATION... and create stunning photos!

30 Practices To Master Aperture, Shutter Speed & ISO In A Day Or Less

The method used by photography schools. Forget about paying expensive photography schools, this is the book you'll ever need to master exposure.

COPYRIGHT 2020

ALL RIGHTS RESERVED, NO PART OF THIS PUBLICATION MAY BE REPRODUCED OR TRANSMITTED IN ANY FORM OR BY ANY MEANS, INCLUDING PHOTOCOPYING, RECORDING OR OTHER ELECTRONIC OR MECHANICAL METHODS, WITHOUT THE PRIOR WRITTEN PERMISSION OF THE PUBLISHER, EXCEPT IN THE CASE OF BRIEF QUOTATIONS EMBODIED IN CRITICAL REVIEWS AND CERTAIN OTHER NONCOMMERCIAL USES PERMITTED BY COPYRIGHT LAW.

Prologue	4
Let's start out with the basics	5
Aperture:	6
Shutter speed:	7
ISO:	8
Then What is Exposure?	8
How exposure affects your pictures	8
So what is a correct exposure?	9
What is Overexposure?	10
What is Underexposure?	11
What is Manual Exposure?	11
Exposure Triangle	12
Exposure Triangle elements trade-offs	15
Shutter Speed	15
ISO	18
Aperture	19
What is f-number?	19
What is Depth of Field?	20
What is shallow depth of field?	20
What is a Large Depth of Field?	21
You have only two questions to ask yourself	25
The exposure bucket analogy	27
Manual Mode Easy Guide:	29
Examples	30
Sports Photographer	30
Portrait Photographer	30
What the Light Meter Does	32
Understanding Histograms	33
How to Read the Histogram	33
Histogram Exposure Chart	34
Underexposure	34
Exposed to the left	34
Ideal Exposure	34

Exposed to the Right	35
Overexposure	35
Knowing your camera For Practices	**36**
Adjusting Aperture in Canon Camera	36
Adjusting Aperture in Nikon Camera	37
Adjusting Shutter Speed	38
Nikon camera Screen	38
Canon camera Screen	39
Practices	**40**
Exercises	**56**
Quiz	**65**
Cheat Cheats	**74**
ISO	74
Aperture	75
Shutter Speed	76

Prologue

So, you just bought a new camera or you want a start using the one you bought three years ago, now what?

Use it in Automatic mode right?

I know because it also happened to me, manual mode is intimidating.

But let me tell you one reason why you should use it in manual mode and not in automatic mode, because you or whoever gave you the camera paid a lot!

So you have to exploit the full potential of the camera, and the only way to do it is… yes you guessed it, in manual mode.

In manual mode is the only way you are going to exploit the camera potential and your creativity potential.

This is also the reason why professional photographers ONLY use manual mode because this mode is the only way to fully transmit the idea, intention, emotions, message that the photographer intends to the photograph.

But don't worry, I will guide you through all the concepts in a very simple and painless way, with little reading and more practice so that at the end of this book you will completely dominate the manual mode and all the related concepts, and you will be thinking and speaking like a pro photographer.

But be aware that it will only happen if you compromise and finish all the practices in this book, so think about the money you spent in the camera plus the money you spent in this book and make it worth it!

I know this book only covers the manual mode and there are other concepts pending so you can become a complete pro photographer, but believe me that these concepts are the foundations of every pro photographer, so if you understand and internalize these concepts you will already be a 95% pro photographer.

Let's start out with the basics

It all starts with light. Without light there is no photo.

So the best way to fully understand the concepts and never forget them is to follow the journey of the light through the camera.

This journey will lead you to the famous exposure triangle that will be explained further.

Every camera is basically two different parts. One is the lens and the other is the body (there are two types of cameras, DSLR and mirrorless but it's the same principle).

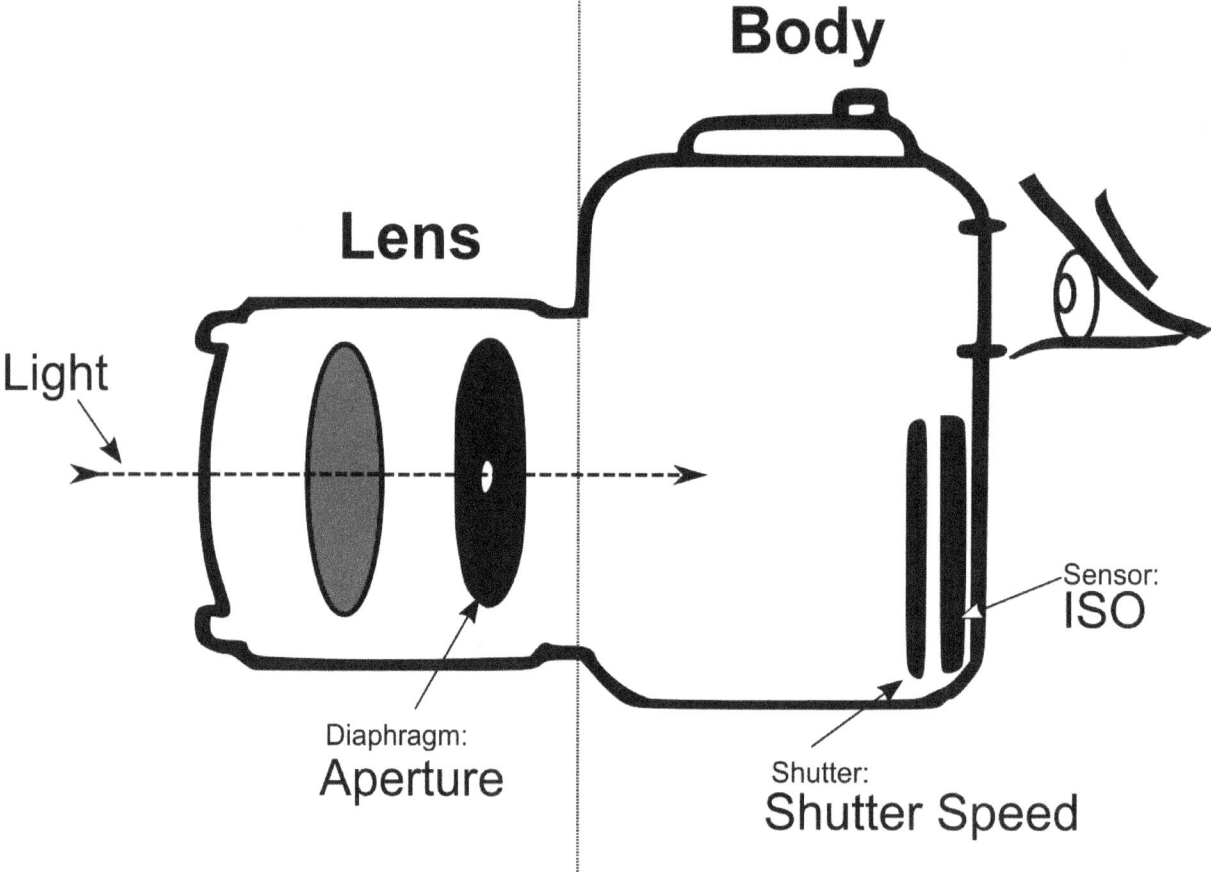

With this diagram we can see three different elements that interact with the light journey, aperture, shutter and ISO, and yes these are the three elements that complete the exposure triangle, which means that these are the only variables of the camera that we can modify to change the exposure of a photo.

Aperture:

Aperture controls the ring inside the lens (diaphragm) which opens and closes to control how much light hits the imaging sensor. The bigger that hole is, it lets more light in through and the smaller it is it will let less light through. Think of it as the pupil in your eye.

Less Light

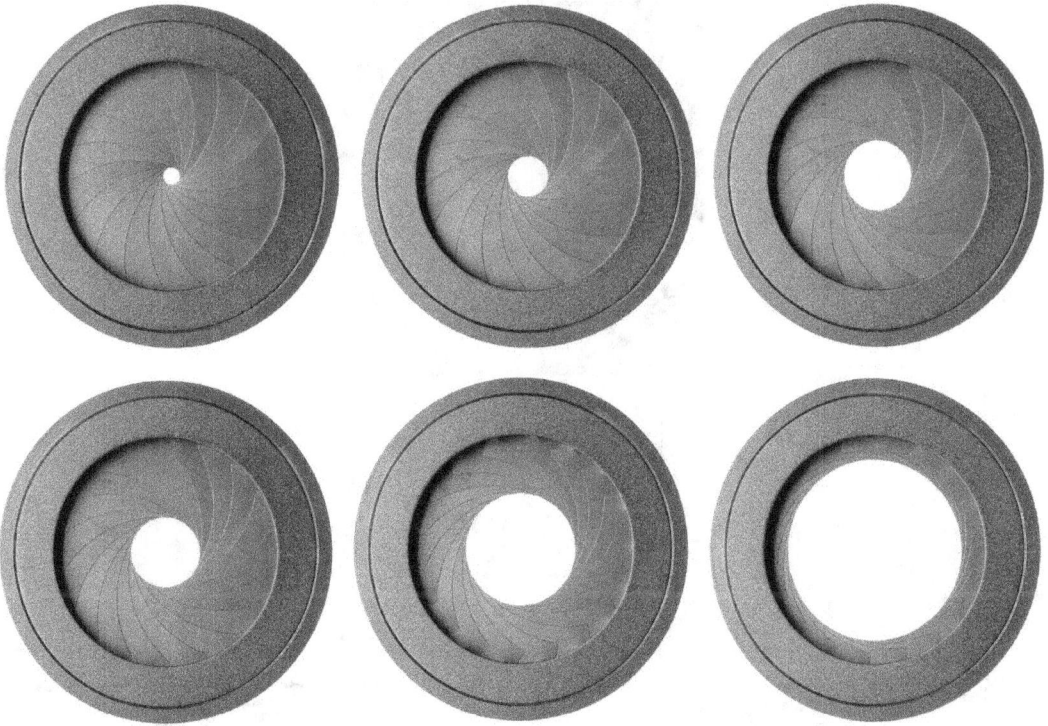

More Light

It is specified in terms of an f-stop value, which can at times be counterintuitive, because the area of the opening increases as the f-stop decreases.

 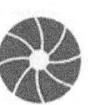 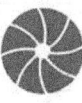

F 5.6   F 8   F 11   F 16

Shutter speed:

Controls the duration that the sensor will be exposed to the light. In front of the sensor there is the shutter that flips up to reveal the sensor for an amount of time. The more time it stays open obviously lets more light through to the sensor to be caught in the image. Shutter speed is denoted in seconds and can go from fractions of a second to 30 seconds. There is also the option called "bulb" which will let the shutter open as long as you maintain the Shutter button oppressed.

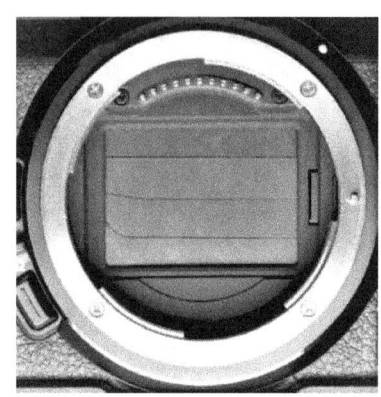

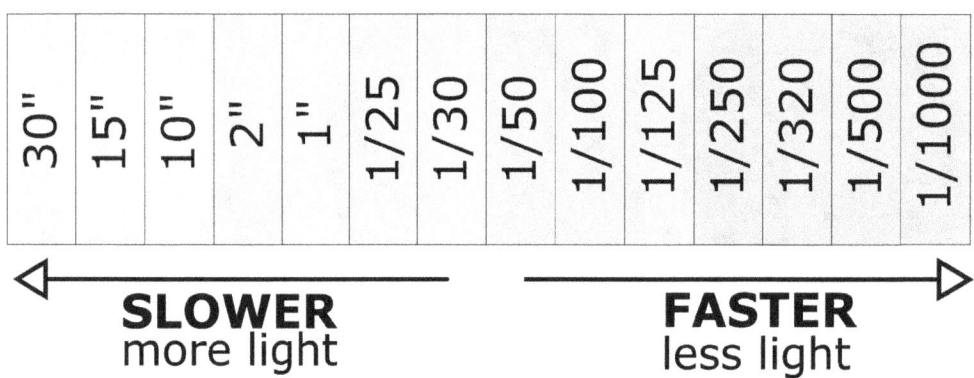

ISO:

Controls the sensitivity of your camera's sensor to light. Is denoted by a number from 100 to 3200 or more.

100... 200... 400... 640... 800... 1600... 3200...

⇐ **LOWER** less sensitive   **HIGHER** more sensitive ⇒

Then What is Exposure?

Exposure is a quantity of light, it's the amount of light that reaches a photosensitive material (i.e. the film or your camera's sensor) to create an image and is determined by a combination of aperture, ISO and shutter speed.

How exposure affects your pictures

A photograph's exposure (the quantity of light you've allowed to capture the sensor) determines how bright or dark your photo is.

The more light captures the sensor the brighter your photo is, and the other way around, the less light you let the sensor capture the darker your photo is.

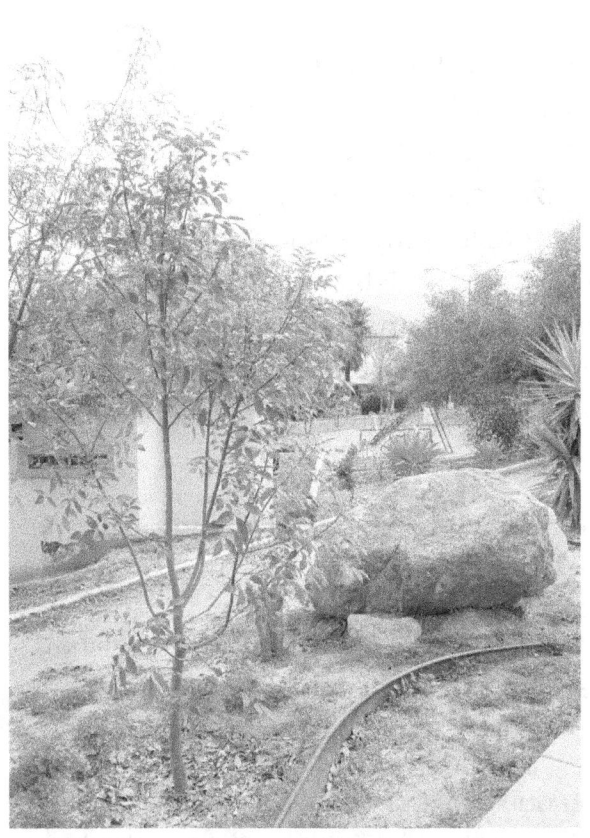

More light captured by the sensor.

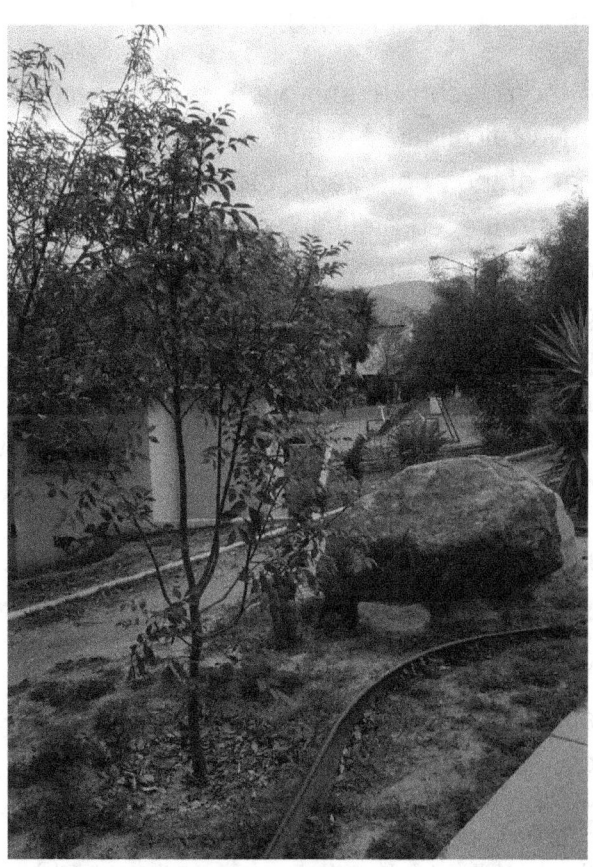

Less light captured by the sensor.

So what is a correct exposure?

Exposure is a quantity of light. Ok, but how much light do I need to expose a photo correctly?

That, my friend, depends on the scene you have in front of you, and the result you want to get. It depends on whether you want to capture more or less detail in the dark (shadows) or bright tones (highlights). In the end, it depends on the story you want to tell.

Therein lies the art of photography. You must exercise the right control over the light that reaches the sensor (or film) to get the image you want.

Then "Correct" exposure may be defined as an exposure that achieves the effect the photographer intended.

A more technical approach recognises that a sensor (or photographic film) has a physically limited useful exposure range, sometimes called dynamic range. If, for any part of the photograph, the actual exposure is outside this range, the sensor cannot record it accurately. In a very simple model, for example, out-of-range values would be recorded as "black" (underexposed) or "white" (overexposed) rather than the precisely graduated shades of colour and tone required to describe "detail". Therefore, the purpose of exposure adjustment is to control the physical amount of light from the subject that is allowed to fall on the sensor, so that 'significant' areas of shadow and highlight detail do not exceed the sensor''s useful exposure range. This ensures that no 'significant' information is lost during capture.

If more light gets to the sensor, you can capture more detail in the dark tones although you may lose detail in the bright ones, and vice versa.

Your goal is to get the level of brightness/darkness you want in the photo. A level that allows you to show through the picture the scene as you see it or want to transmit it. To do that, you have to decide how much light you want to reach the sensor.

Then "correct" exposure is the one in which you don't lose information in the shadows or the highlights. In other words, when nothing is blown out (highlights) or lost in shadow in an image, it has achieved correct exposure.

What is Overexposure?

Overexposure occurs when the camera sensor has been exposed to too much light. Images that are overexposed tend to have very bright images appearing almost white with little or no detail.

A photograph may be described as overexposed when it has a loss of highlight detail, that is, when important bright parts of an image are "washed out" or effectively all white, known as "blown-out highlights" or "clipped whites".

What is Underexposure?

Underexposure refers to when an image is too dark, according to the technical rules of what is considered to be correct exposure, ie, darker than what you remember the original scene to be.

To get around this, you would need to adjust your exposure settings, ie, slow down the shutter speed, increase the aperture size or increase the ISO.

A photograph may be described as underexposed when it has a loss of shadow detail, that is, when important dark areas are "muddy" or indistinguishable from black, known as "blocked-up shadows" (or sometimes "crushed shadows", "crushed blacks", or "clipped blacks").

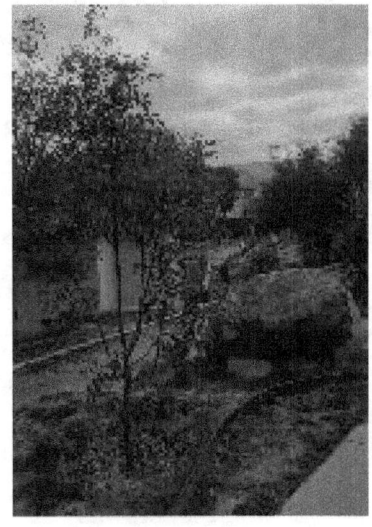
Underexposed

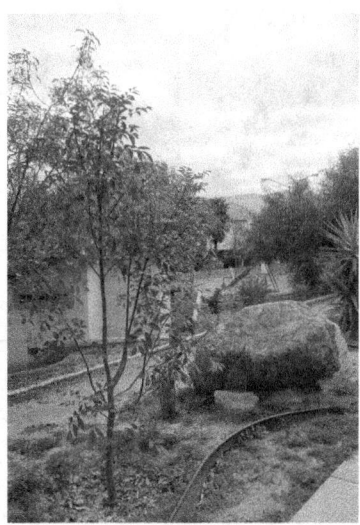
Correct exposure

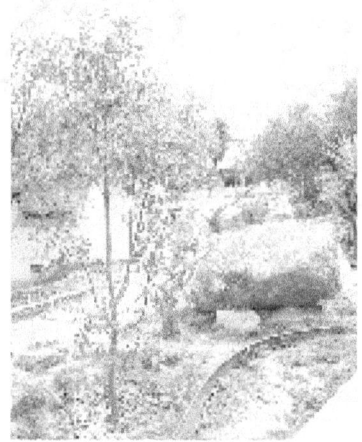
Overexposed

What is Manual Exposure?

Manual Exposure is when the photographer manually sets the aperture, ISO and shutter speed all independently of each other in order to adjust exposure. This gives them full creative control over the output of the image.

Exposure Triangle

So once you know the three elements that make up the exposure (ISO, shutter speed and aperture) you know the basics of your exposure triangle, it's just a case of balancing out these three elements to get the correct exposure to the light.

Normally ISO goes from 100 to 6400 although there are cameras that go way past 6400.

A lower ISO would be a darker exposure and higher ISO would be a lighter exposure.

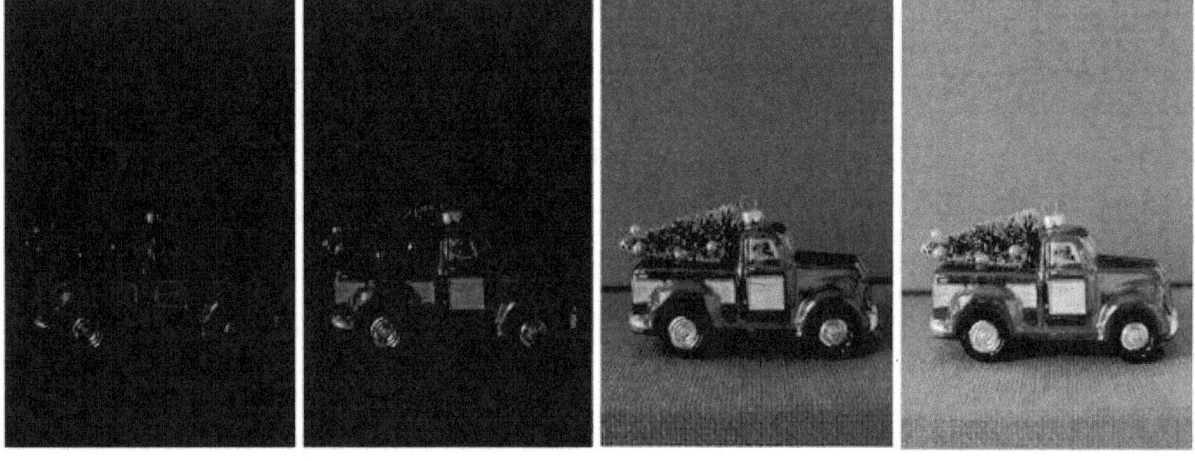

100... 200... 400... 640... 800... 1600... 3200...

For shutter speed a darker exposure would be 1/2000 second, this is a very fast shutter speed that wouldn't let in much light, on the other side,1/50 would let in a lot of light.

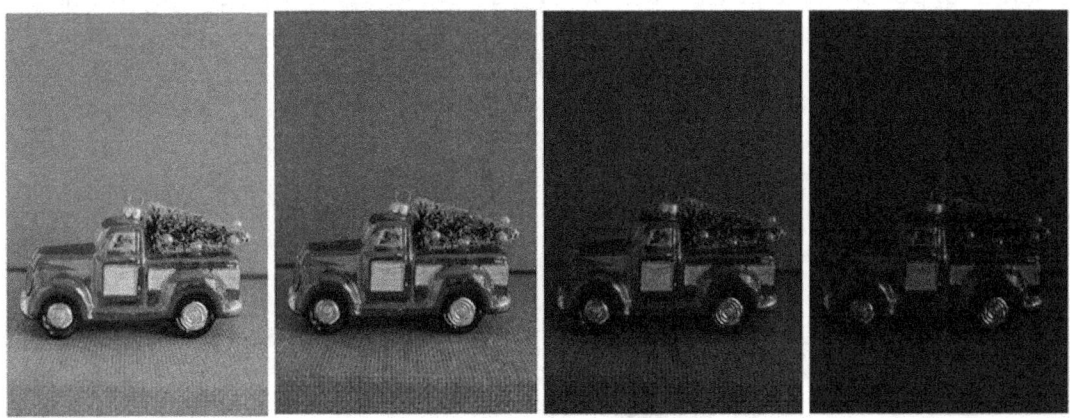

1/50   1/100   1/125   1/250   1/320   1/500   1/1000   1/2000

For aperture f/16 is a very very small aperture opening that wouldn't bring in much light and on the other end F 5.6 that's quite a wide aperture opening that would bring in much light.

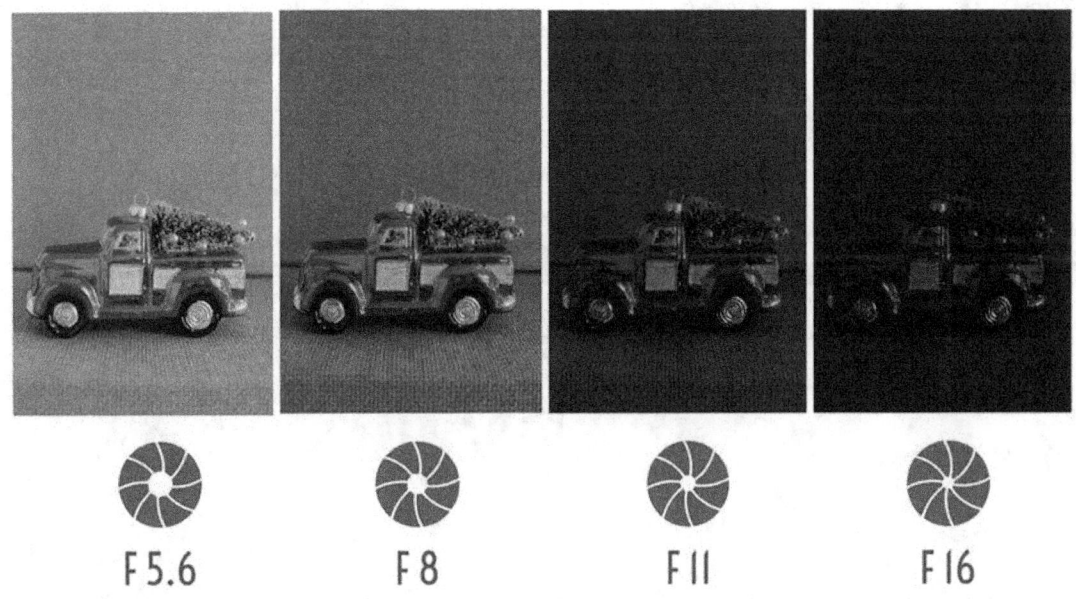

F 5.6   F 8   F 11   F 16

To create any exposure all you have to do is balance these three elements against each other so if you want more light you could bump ISO up, you could slow shutter speed down or you could open up aperture any of those three.

If you look at exposure let's say it's too bright you could darken it down by closing down aperture by speeding up shutter speed or by dropping ISO those three options.

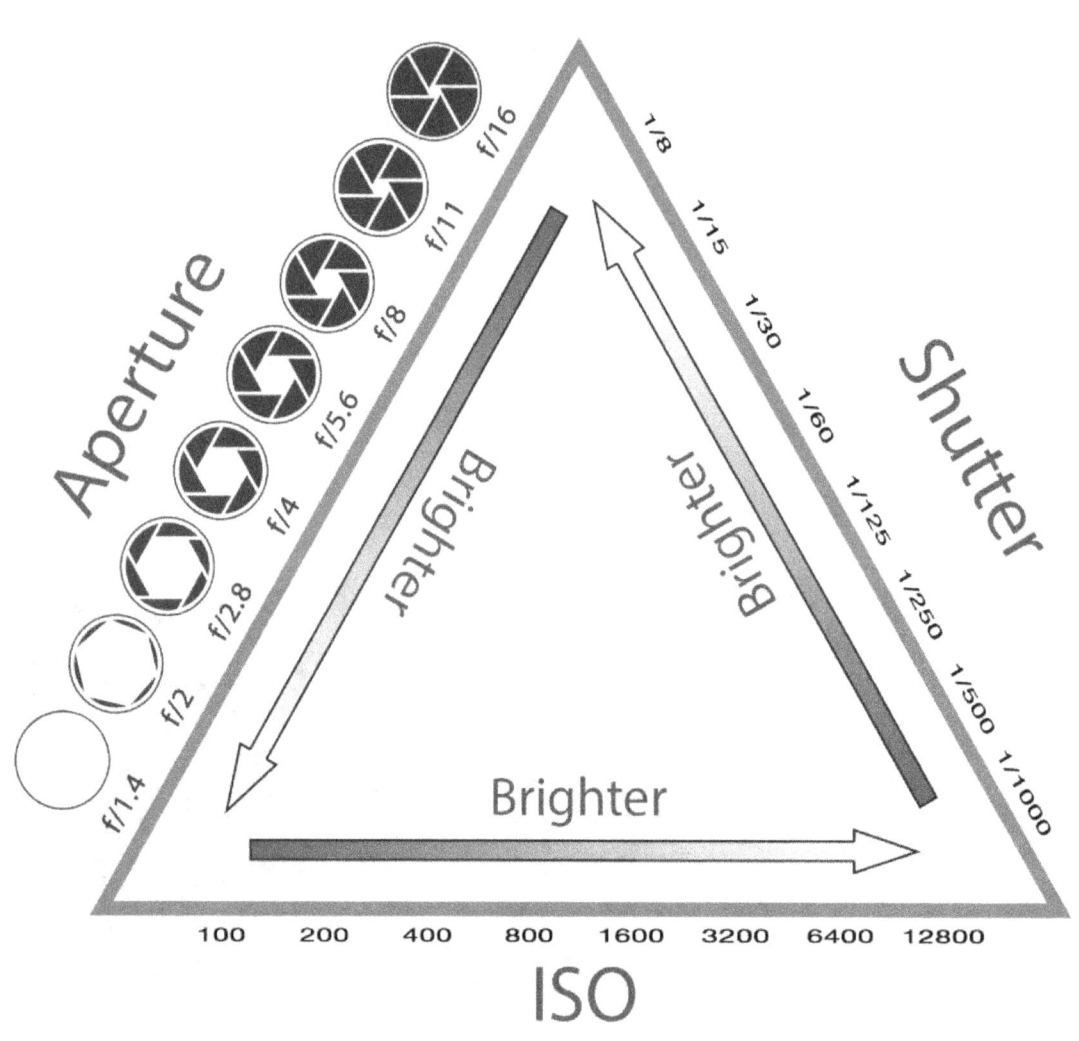

Exposure Triangle elements trade-offs

All you need to know to make a good exposure is what the trade-offs are for each of these elements.

Shutter Speed

For shutter speed the trade-off is movement and that just means that when you slow down or speed up your shutter speed what it's going to do is affect how movement appears, here if you shoot something with 8 seconds shutter speed it's going to blur on the other side a 1/8000 second it's going to freeze your motion.

So all you need to know when you are playing with your shutter speed is that the slower your shutter speed is going to blur motion and the faster your shutter speed is going to freeze. That's the trade-off for shutter speed.

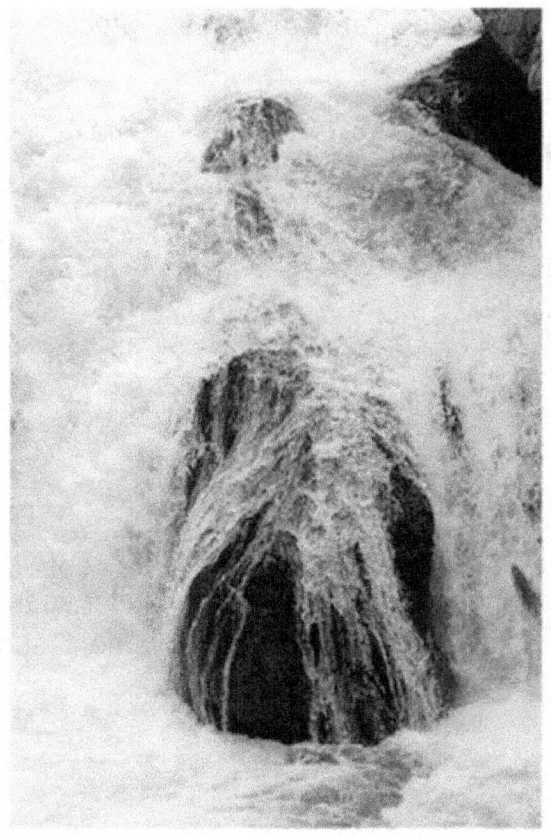
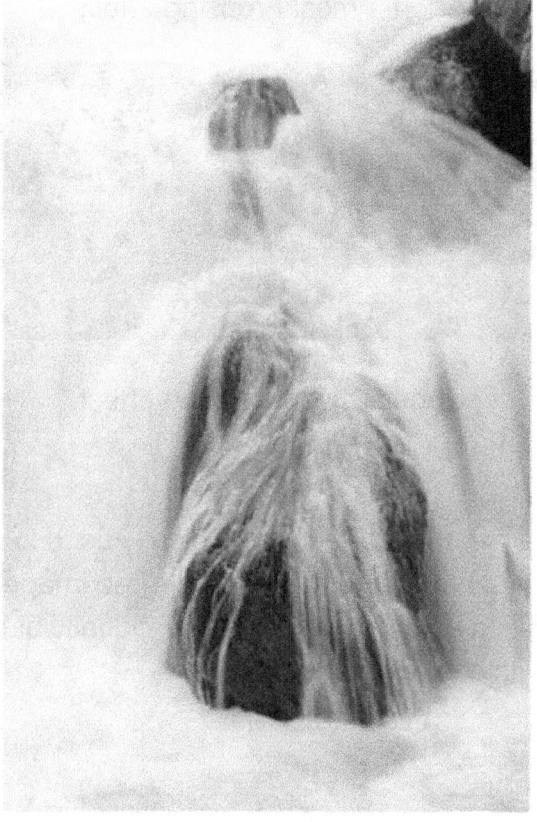

Short Times: Freezing effect   Long Time: movement effect

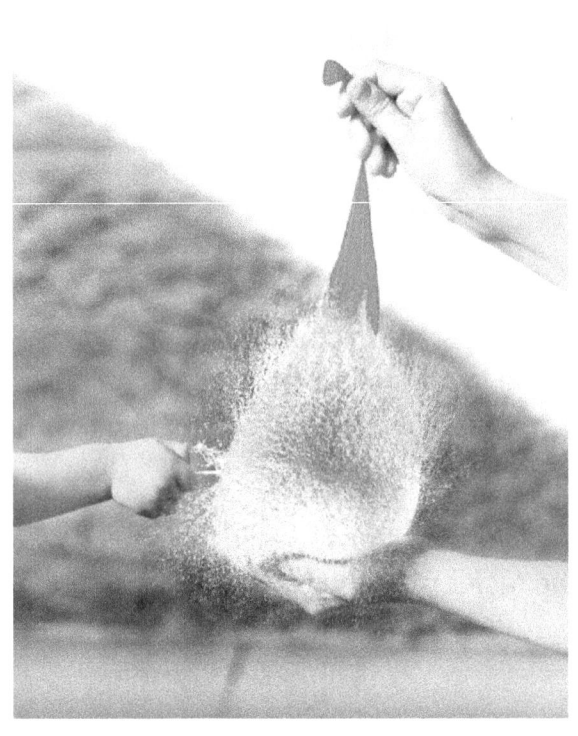 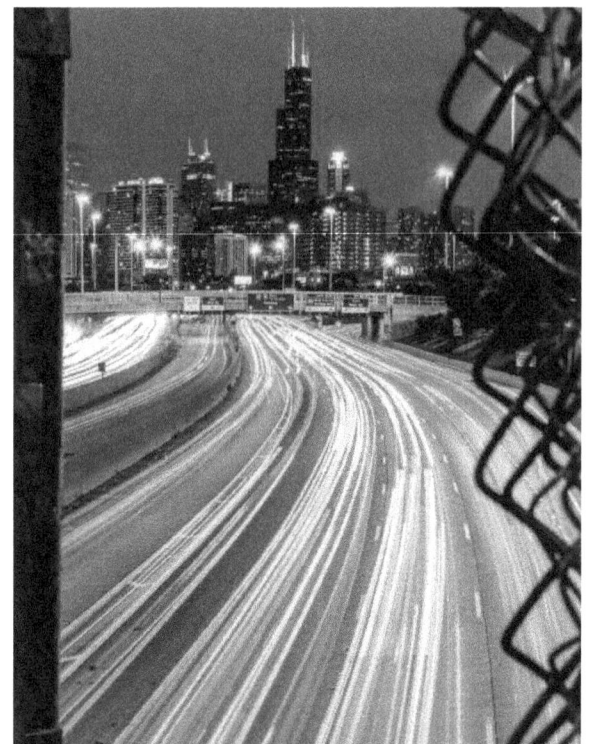

Short Times: Freezing effect   Long Time: movement effect

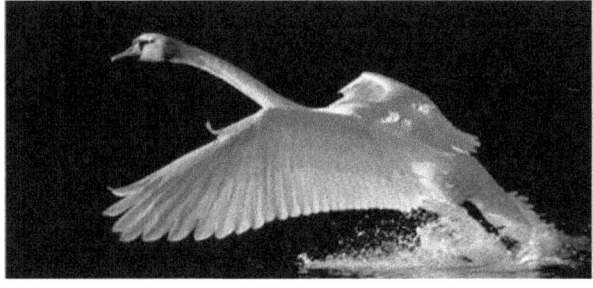 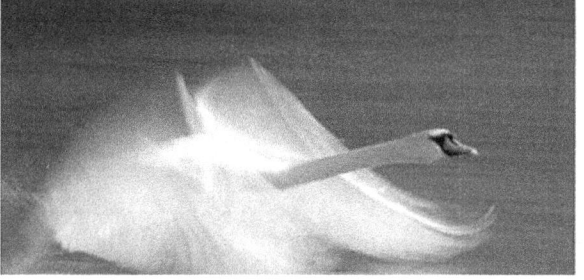

Short Times: Freezing effect   Long Time: movement effect

Faster shutter speeds are typically used in sports photography, or any situation where you want to create a sharp, blur-free image. On the other hand, slower shutter speeds are used when you want to intentionally blur a subject to capture the movement, such as with exploding fireworks.

Commonly, shutter speeds are adjusted in increments that have a halving or doubling relationship, ie., every time you adjust the shutter speed, you are either halving the shutter speed, or doubling it. As with adjusting aperture – or ISO Speed for that matter – these increments are known as 'stops'.

The important thing to bear in mind with shutter speed is that whenever you increase the shutter speed by a full 'stop', you are halving the amount of light that passes through to the imaging sensor. To compensate, you would need to increase the size of the aperture, or increase the ISO by a full stop. Be aware that this will change the image, either by narrowing the depth of field, or by increasing grain in the image.

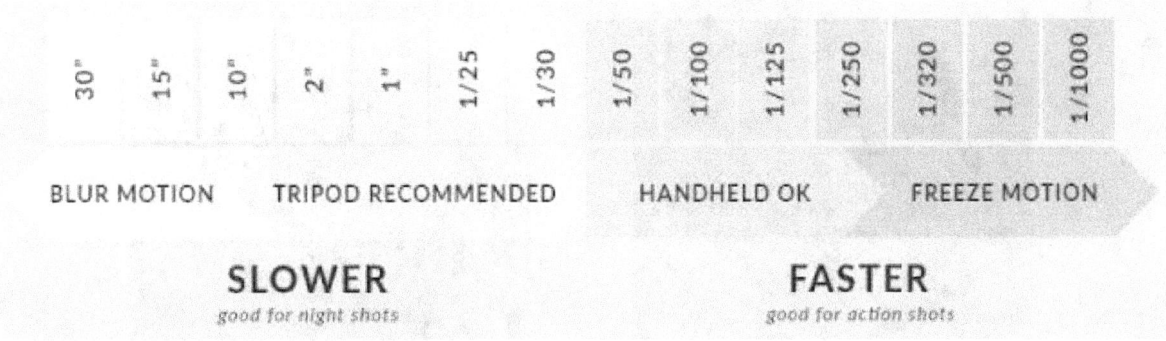

Shutter Speed	Typical Examples
1 - 30+ seconds	Specialty night and low-light photos on a tripod
2 - 1/2 second	To add a silky look to flowing water Landscape photos on a tripod for enhanced depth of field
1/2 to 1/30 second	To add motion blur to the background of a moving subject Carefully taken hand-held photos with stabilization
1/50 - 1/100 second	Typical hand-held photos without substantial zoom
1/250 - 1/500 second	To freeze everyday sports/action subject movement Hand-held photos with substantial zoom (telephoto lens)
1/1000 - 1/4000 second	To freeze extremely fast, up-close subject motion

ISO

ISO trade-off is noise, an ISO of 6400 is going to give you a high amount of noise in your image, an ISO of 100 it's going to give you a low amount of noise in your image, so if you rise ISO you will be bringing more digital noise into your image, that is ISOs trade-off.

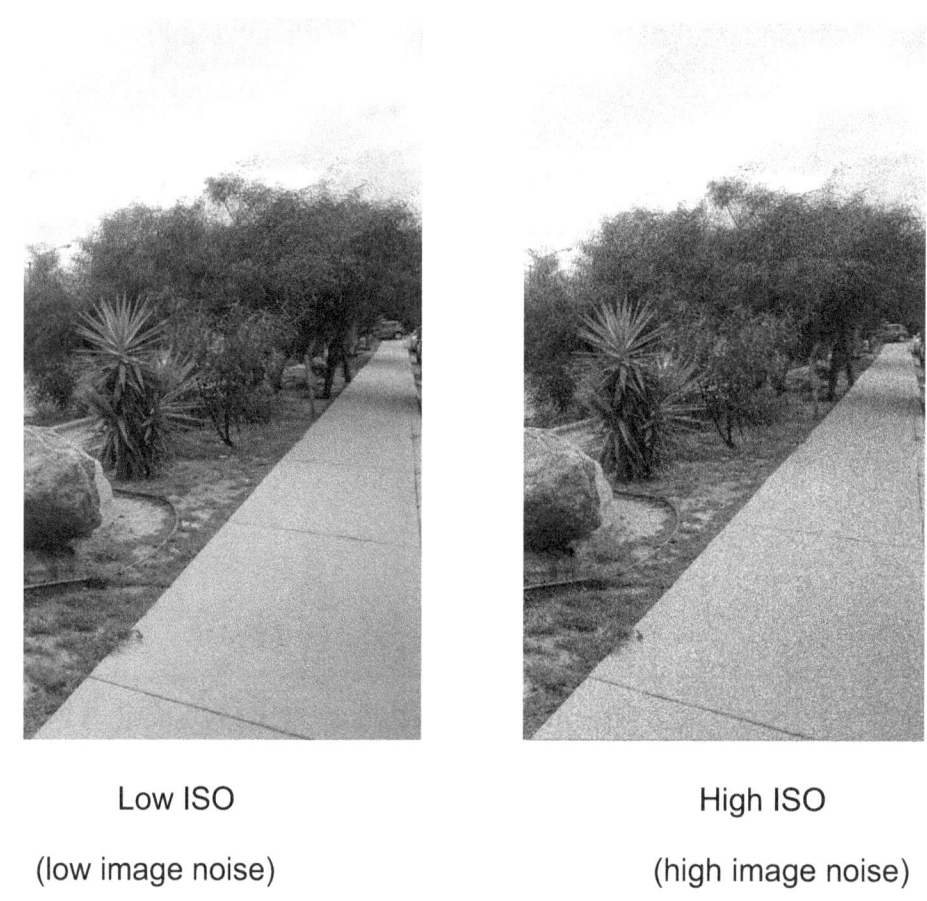

Low ISO　　　　　　　　　　　　　　　　High ISO

(low image noise)　　　　　　　　　　　(high image noise)

Note: image noise is also known as "film grain" in traditional film photography

A lower ISO is almost always desirable, since higher ISO dramatically increases image noise. As a result, ISO is usually only increased from its minimum value if the desired aperture and shutter speed aren't otherwise obtainable.

Aperture

Aperture is going to introduce depth of field. Depth of field means how much of your image is actually going to be in focus, you might want a very shallow depth of field if you're shooting a portrait with just the front of the faces in focus and everything else is blurred or a landscape photographer might want a very deep depth of field to keep everything in focus.

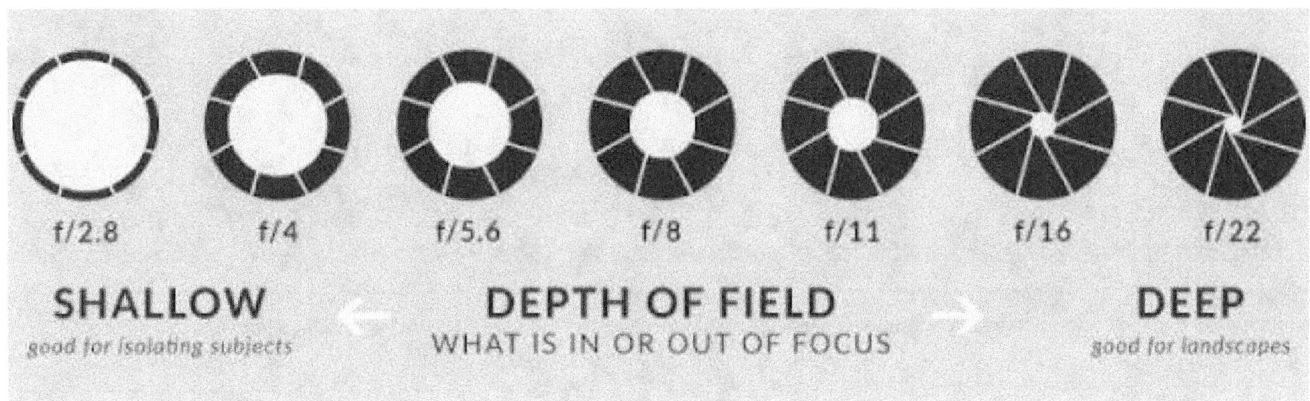

At f-22 you're going to get a deeper depth of field then you would down at f-1.4 which is going to give you a shallow depth of field.

What is f-number?

In photography, aperture is shown through an f-number, or f-stop. The smaller the number, the wider the lens is opened allowing more light in, such as f/2.8. The larger equals less light, such as f/16.

What is Depth of Field?

Depth of Field (DoF) is the range in front or behind the point of focus where objects remain sharp and in focus. The wider the aperture (lower f-number), the shallower the DoF. As such, depth of field plays a crucial part in the look and feel of an image.

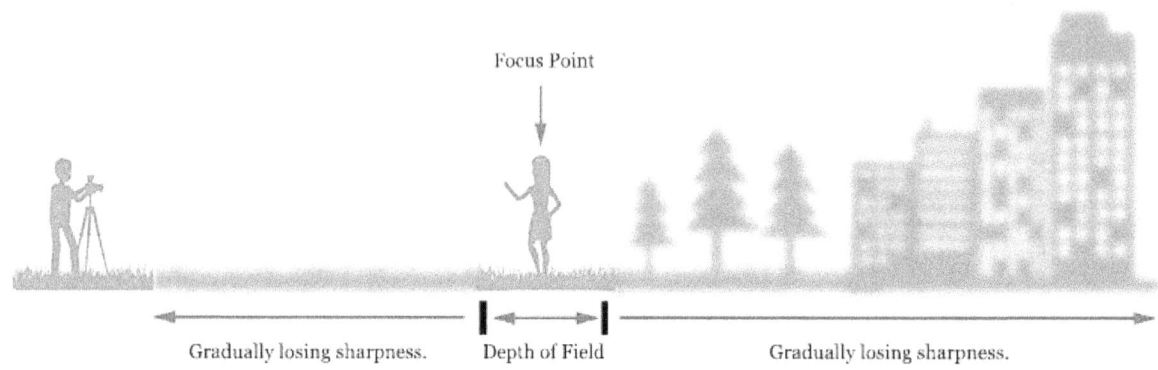

What is shallow depth of field?

A small or shallow depth of field (DoF) means a smaller range of focus. The wider the aperture (lower f-number), the shallower the DoF. A shallow DoF means you can deliberately blur out details in either the background or foreground of the scene, allowing you to draw the viewer's attention to one particular subject or part of your scene.

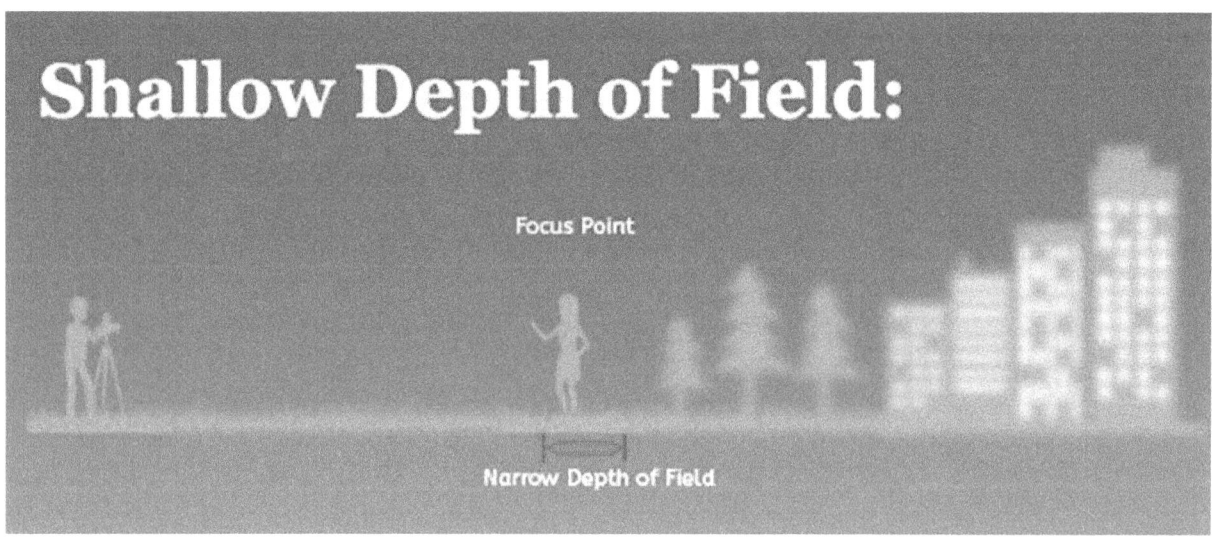

A shallow or small DOF might be used when only a small amount of the image is in sharp focus while blurring any background or surrounding areas in view that could distract the viewer's attention. Therefore, a shallow DOF is good for close ups of faces and creating a sense of intimacy around the focal point within your shot.

What is a Large Depth of Field?

A large depth of field (DOF) means a greater range of the scene is in focus, as opposed to a shallow depth of field when only part of the scene is in focus. To achieve a large depth of field, you would use a small aperture. Landscape photography generally uses large depth of field to make sure close objects as well as objects further away, are sharp and in focus.

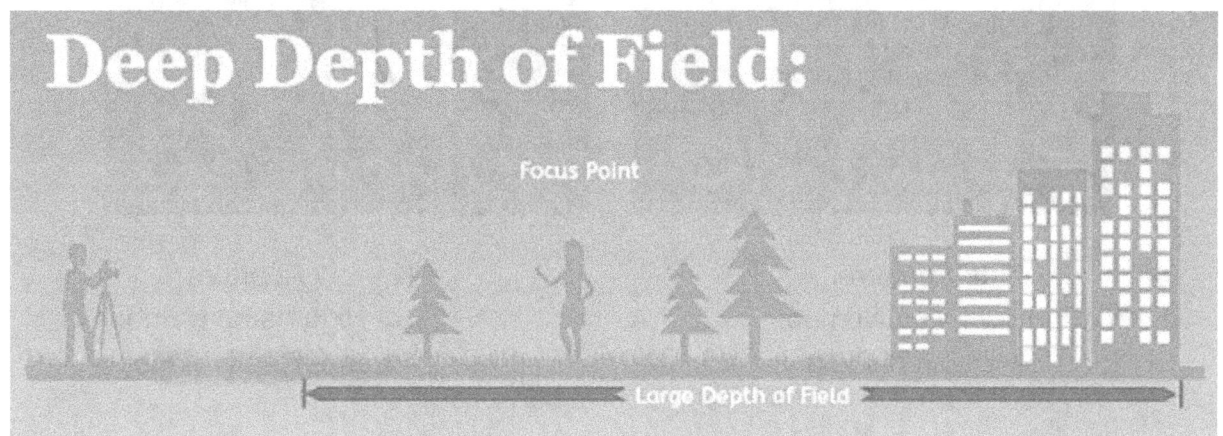

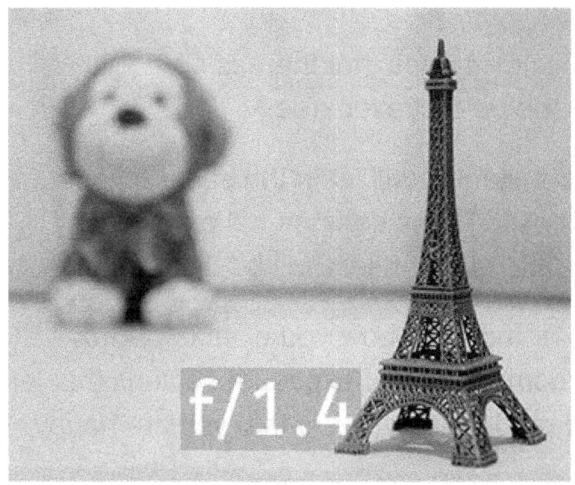
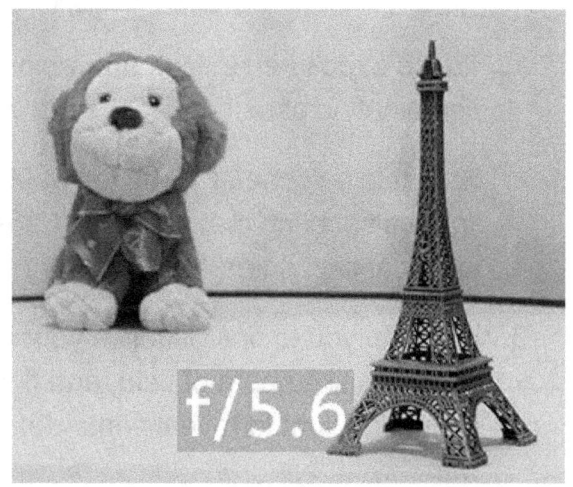

Wide Aperture
f/1.4 - Low f-stop Number
Shallow Depth of Field

Narrow Aperture
f/5.6 - High f-stop Number
Large Depth of Field

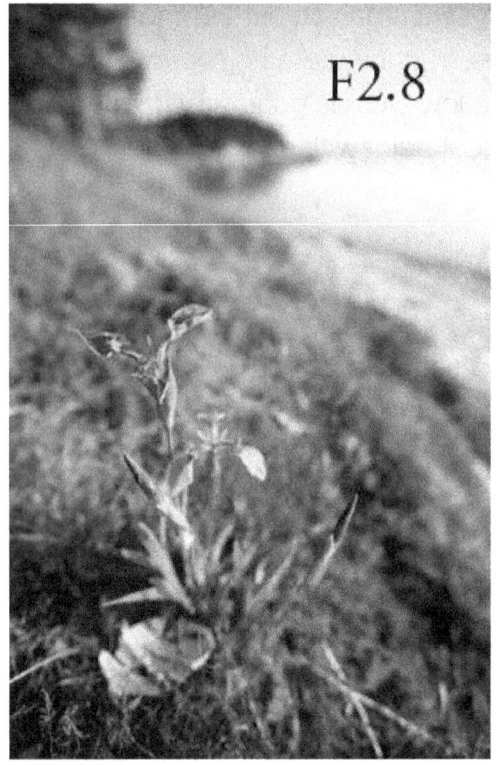 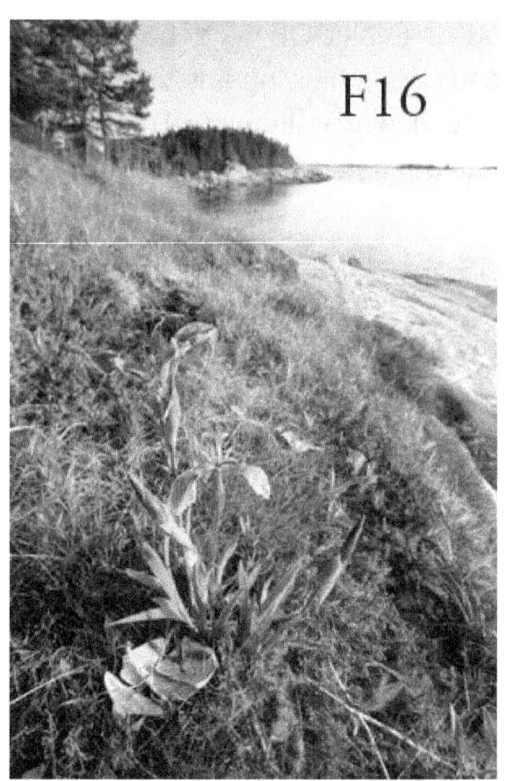

Wide Aperture
f/2.8 - Low f-stop Number
Shallow Depth of Field

Narrow Aperture
f/16 - High f-stop Number
Large Depth of Field

1. These exposure settings are reciprocal, which means that there is no single combination of settings that will give you the perfect exposure.

2. Shooting a scene at 1/100sec at f/5.6, for instance, will let in the same amount of light as shooting that scene at 1/25sec at f/11. These settings will produce identical exposures, but of course things like depth of field will be different.

3. It's up to you to pre-visualise your image and decide how you want to portray elements like depth of field, and find the combination of exposure settings that let in enough light to reveal some detail and render rich colours that you are happy with.

One can therefore use many combinations of the above three settings to achieve the same exposure. The key, however, is knowing which trade-offs to make, since each setting also influences other image properties. For example, aperture affects depth of field, shutter speed affects motion blur and ISO speed affects image noise.

The next few sections will describe how each setting is specified, what it looks like, and how a given camera exposure mode affects their combination.

Putting it all Together: The Exposure Triangle

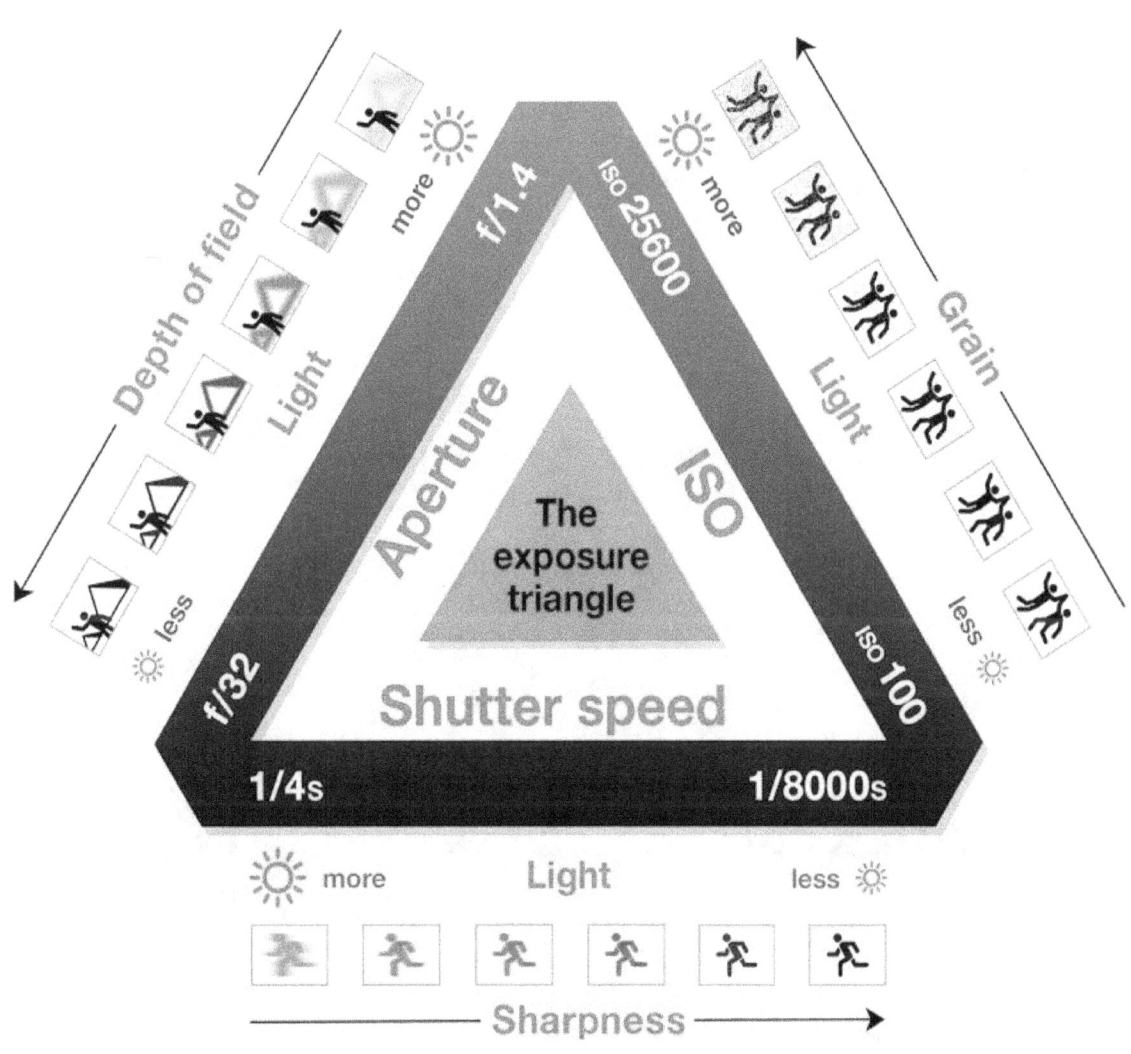

DARKER

SHUTTER	APERTURE	ISO
LESS MOTION BLUR	**BACKGROUND SHARP**	**LESS GRAINY**
1/4000		100
1/2000	f22	
1/1000	f16	200
1/500	f11	400
1/250		
1/125	f8	500
1/60	f5.6	640
1/30	f4	800
1/15		
1/8	f2.8	1000
1/4	f2	1250
1/2		
1	f1.4	1600
2		
MORE MOTION BLUR	**BACKGROUND BLURRY**	**MORE GRAINY**

LIGHTER

You have only two questions to ask yourself

So when we are deciding:

- Should I darken things down by closing down my aperture, I'm gonna deepen my depth of field.

- Should I darken things down by speeding up my shutter speed, I'm gonna freeze action.

- Should I darken things down by lowering my ISO, that's great because there's gonna be less noise in the image.

- If I want to brighten things up with my aperture I'm going to shallow up my depth of field.

- I need to be aware that if I slow down my shutter speed to brighten things up I need to be aware that movement is going to start to blur more.

- And if I open up my ISO to brighten things up I need to be aware that I might be introducing more noise.

When you understand each of these three things are going to control your exposure and each have their trade-offs. Once you know what those trade-offs are you can start to make decisions, because maybe you want to blur the movement, maybe you want to shell out your depth of field and within all of this you're also going to get exactly the correct exposure that you want to achieve.

That might sound a little bit complicated, but actually it leaves you with only two questions to ask yourself before any photo you want to take:

1. What depth of field do you want?

Shallow or Deep

2. How do you want movement to appear?

Frozen or Blurred

Why only two questions?

Because the third question would be how much noise do you want in your image?

And this question makes no sense because we always want as little noise as possible, so ISO should always be as low as possible.

So in terms of the creative aspect of the photograph these are the two questions you're going to use and they're going to inform how you balance those three elements to get the correct exposure.

① Depth of Field
- Shallow - Aperture f/1.4
- Deep - Aperture f/22

② Movement
- Freeze - Shutter Speed 1/1000
- Blur - Shutter Speed 1/60

③ Noise - ISO as low as possible

The exposure bucket analogy

Three variables control exposure, and therefore the amount of light that creates the image in the camera's sensor. To understand how these factors work together, it can help to think of controlling exposure as filling a glass with water.

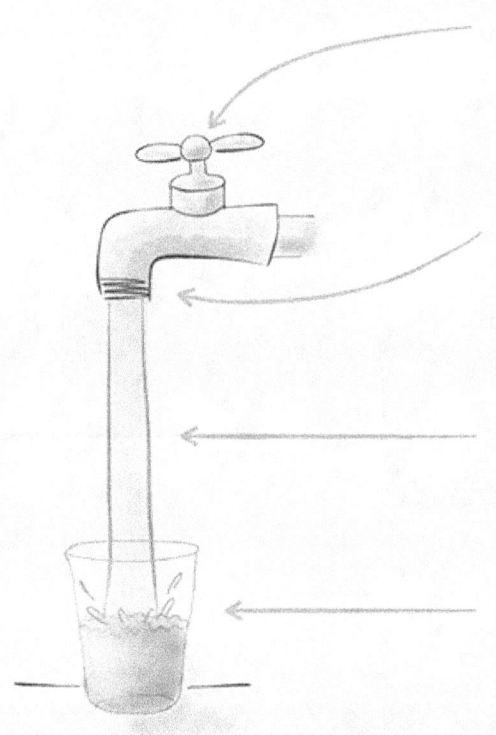

Aperture
How opened or closed is the faucet. This will control the flow of the water (light).

Shutter Speed
The amount of time the faucet is left open. You can fill the glass with a short time if you full open the faucet or with a longer time if you open it just a little bit.

Intensity of Light
The water pressure. If the pressure is high you don't need to full open the faucet or for so long to fill the glass.

ISO
The size of the glass. A small glass (high ISO) will fill more quickly than a big one, but with less info (water/light).

While the water pressure inside the pipeline is uncontrollable, three factors remain under your control: the size of the glass, the duration you leave the tap open, and how many times you turn the tap. You just need to ensure you don't collect too little ("underexposed"), but that you also don't collect too much ("overexposed"). The key is that there are many different combinations of size, time and turns of the tap that will achieve this. For example, for the same quantity of water, you can get away with less time open if you pick a small glass. Alternatively, for the same duration left open, a big glass can be used as long as you plan on getting by with less water.

In photography, the exposure settings of aperture, shutter speed and ISO are analogous to the turns of the tap, time, and size discussed above. Furthermore, just as the water pressure inside the pipeline was beyond your control above, so too is natural light for a photographer.

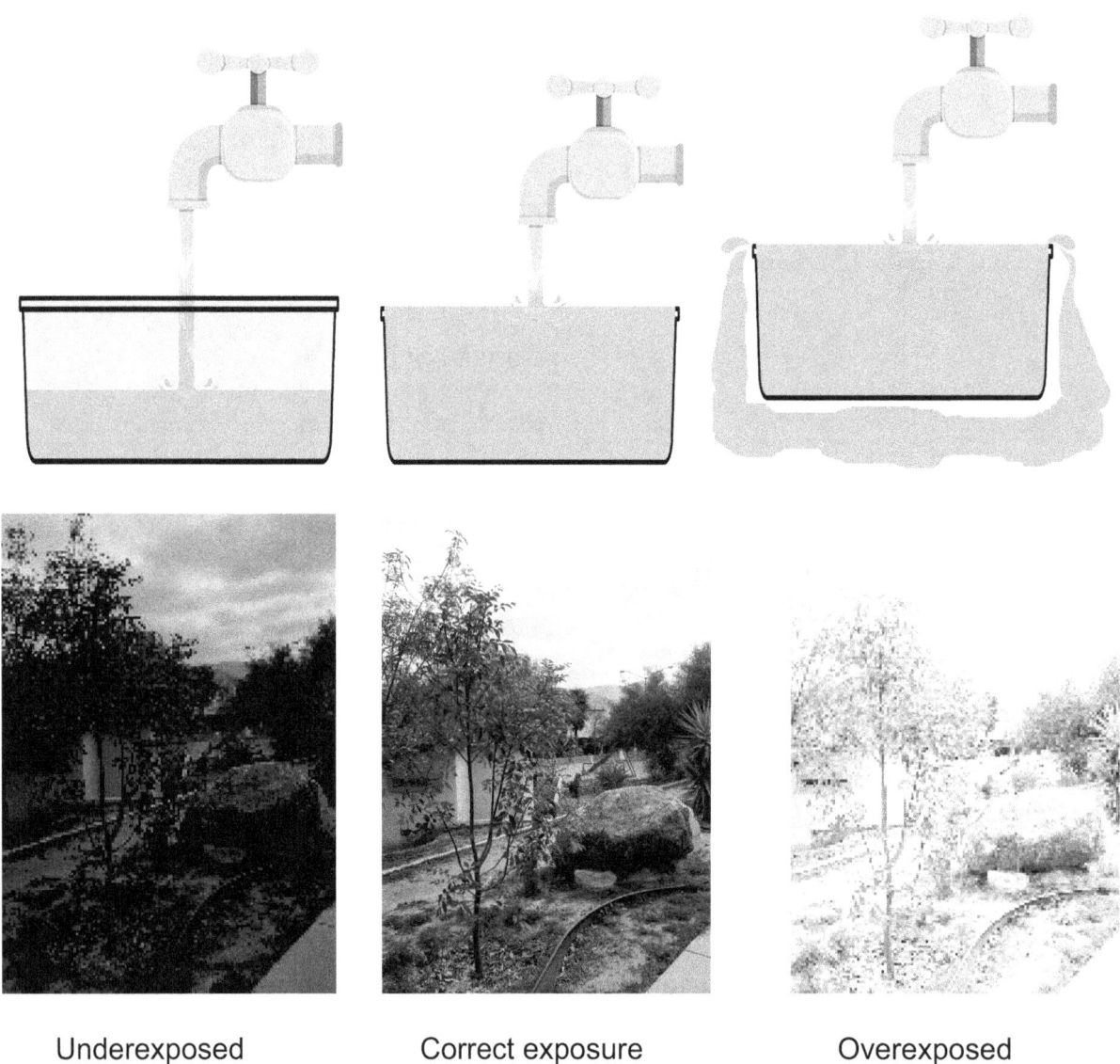

Underexposed   Correct exposure   Overexposed

Manual Mode Easy Guide:

1. **Set ISO**

    100   Sunny
    400   Cloudy
    800   Indoor
    3200 Dark/Night

2. **Ask yourself, is more important Motion or Depth of field?**

If Motion is more important set Shutter speed first, if Depth of field is more important set Aperture first.

   For Shutter Speed

    1/2 - 1/8   Blur Motion
    1/125   Portraits
    1/250   Freeze Motion
    1/500+   Sports and Extreme Motion

*Slow shutter = Blurred motion
*Fast shutter = Freezed action

   For Aperture

    1.2 - 3.5   Very blurry background (Portraits, Bokeh)
    3.5 - 6.3   Slightly blurry background
    6.3 - 22   Wide DOF (Landscapes)

3. **Adjust the other element (Shutter Speed or Aperture) accordingly.**
   - Watch the light meter in the bottom of the viewfinder and adjust the other variable (Shutter Speed or Aperture) until the light meter is at 0.
   - Review the image on the LCD and check the histogram to see that the tones are evenly distributed across the graph.

4. **If (Only If) the adjustment of the other element is not enough to create a correct exposure, readjust ISO.**

Examples

Let's take two different photographers, one is going to be a sports photographer, the second is going to be a portrait photographer.

1. Sports Photographer

So your sports photographer is gonna ask himself those two questions: what do I want my depth of field to be and what do I want my shutter speed to be.

But shutter speed in his case is going to be way more important because motion is more important than depth of field because he's shooting a soccer game and there's lots of stuff moving around and he wants to freeze that action as happening.

He's going to select something like 1/4000 second to freeze that action, then he's gonna put ISO as low as possible because it's a daytime game so he's gonna be able to get away with ISO 100.

For aperture he selects f/4, he checks exposure and everything looks good but he notices that is too shallow depth of field and it lets a lot of action out of focus and he needs to deepen that depth of field out, so he decides to go to f/8.

Then he is going to bump up his ISO to compensate because closing aperture down is gonna let in less light in, he needs to make his ISO more sensitive to compensate for that, as he wants to keep that most important thing which is his movement frozen.

2. Portrait Photographer

Let's say a portrait photographer is in a studio and he decides f2.8 to be the depth of field as he knows the most important thing is depth of field first because he is shooting portraits.

Now he's going to have to work out his exposure. As he is in a studio with very good lighting, he can get his ISO down as low as possible to keep the noise out, so he sets ISO 100.

But that's going to give him for example let's say 1/10 second shutter speed, and that this speed is introducing some shake in the camera hand holding and the subject moving around slightly introducing slight amount of blur and the thing isn't as sharp as it should be.

So now how does he get this to a better shutter speed that's gonna freeze that action a little bit more and not give him a blurry image or with with handshake so let's say he takes it to 1/100 second he needs to now bump his ISO up to compensate because he's given himself a faster shutter speed, he needs to increase his ISO to make it more sensitive to capture the light that's been lost by the fact that this shutter speed is firing faster and his most important element here is his depth of field that's where he starts.

	AP	SS	ISO
Sports (SS)	f8	1/4000	400
Portrait (AP)	f2.8	1/100	100

That's the question he's going to answer for himself and any photographer. If they are balancing these three elements with each, they're starting with those two questions: what do I want my movement to look like and what do I want my depth of field to be. Keep the ISO as low as possible.

What the Light Meter Does

The light meter is an internal function of the camera that gives you a visual indication of how dark or light the image is according to the camera. The light meter is this little thing you see in Live View or through the viewfinder:

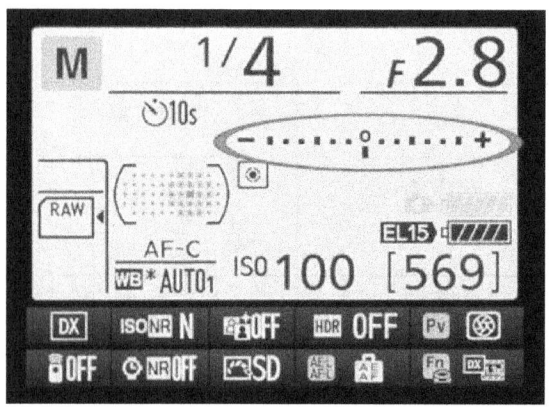
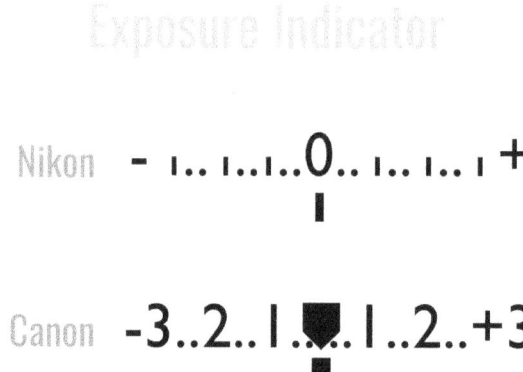

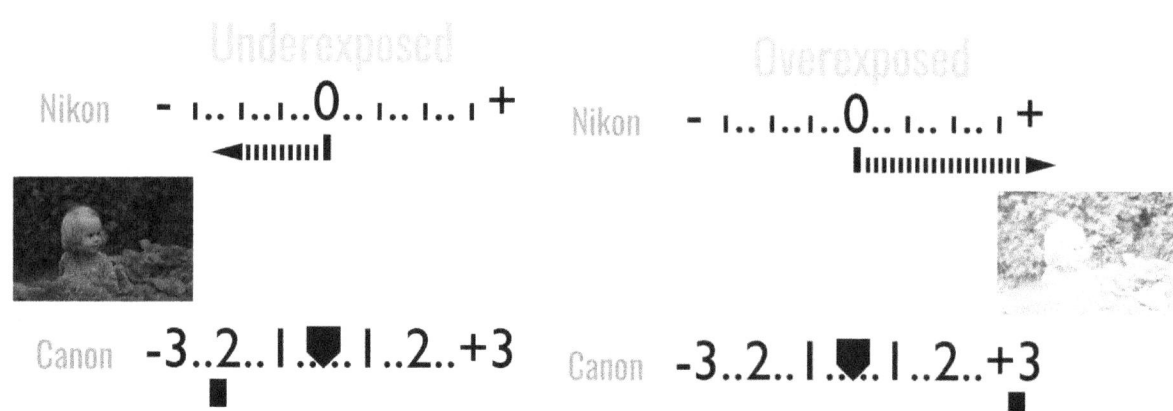

When the white cursor is at zero, this means according to the camera's internal algorithm, that's the right exposure. A deviation to the left means the image is darker, and if the white cursor is to the right, the image is lighter.

The light meter sees a scene (the picture you point the camera to) as points with different brightness as if the image was all black and white. Each point is evaluated against the camera's zero.

Understanding Histograms

The camera converts the images to grayscale and divides it into 256 levels of brightness:

Starting at 0 (pure black) and up to 256 (pure white). With this data the camera creates a graph called the Histogram.

How to Read the Histogram

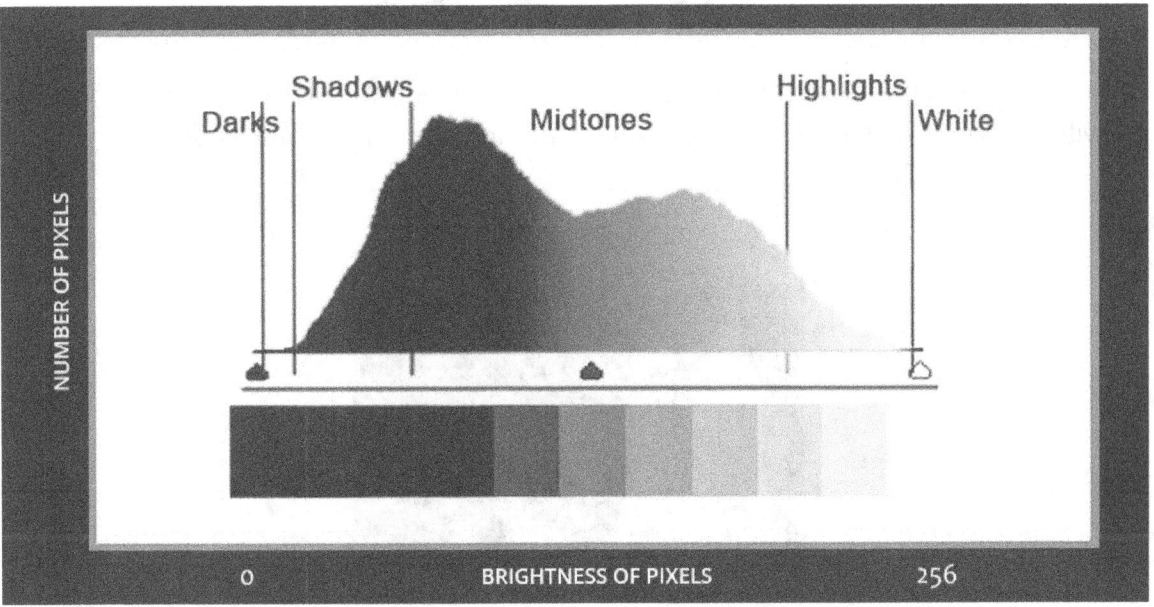

The pixels close to the left edge of the histogram are equal to 0% brightness and pixels close to the right edge are equal to 100% brightness. The vertical axis of the histogram symbolizes the number of pixels that are in that tone.

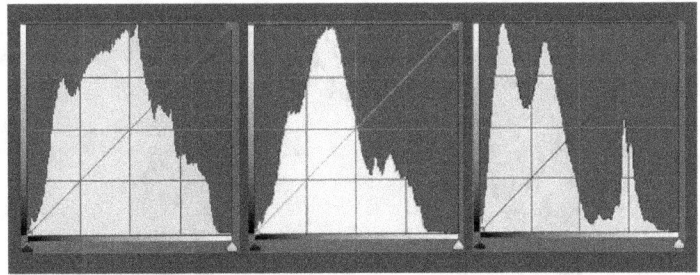

The RGB histogram (red, green, blue) shows the color you captured and displays as three separate graphs or all three colors overlaid on a single graph.

Histogram Exposure Chart

Underexposure

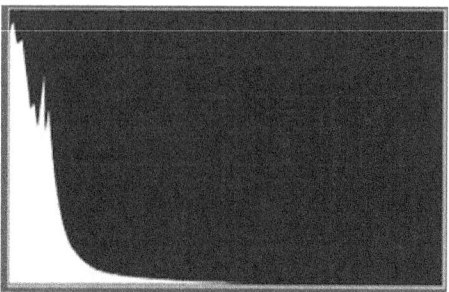

This is a very dark photo, most likely shot at night. It is almost sure it will be impossible to fix with edition. You'll need to take another photo with longer shutter speed.

Exposed to the left

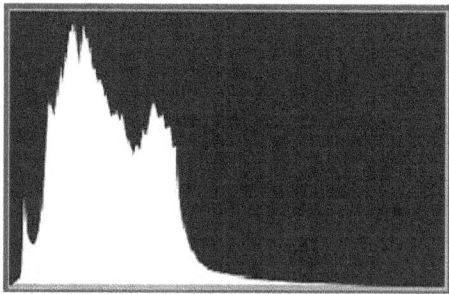

This is a slightly dark photo, still you can consider it a normal histogram. But you can do better if you increase shutter speed.

Ideal Exposure

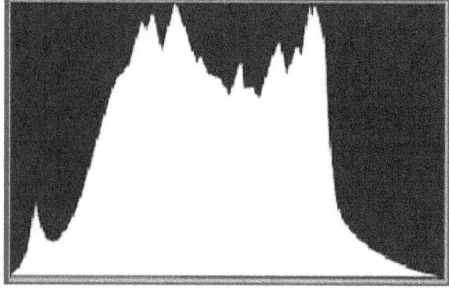

Most people will say that the exposure to the right is perfect. But thi is really an ideal histogram, and it does not need to be fixed.

Exposed to the Right

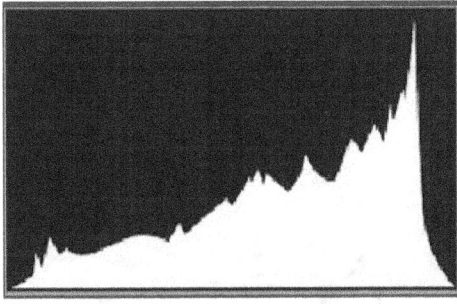

This is the best histogram. You will need minimal corrections during post-processing.

Overexposure

This is a broken photo, impossible to fix. You lost most of the information in highlights. You will need to take another photo.

Knowing your camera For Practices

1. Adjusting Aperture in Canon Camera
   a. Push Av button

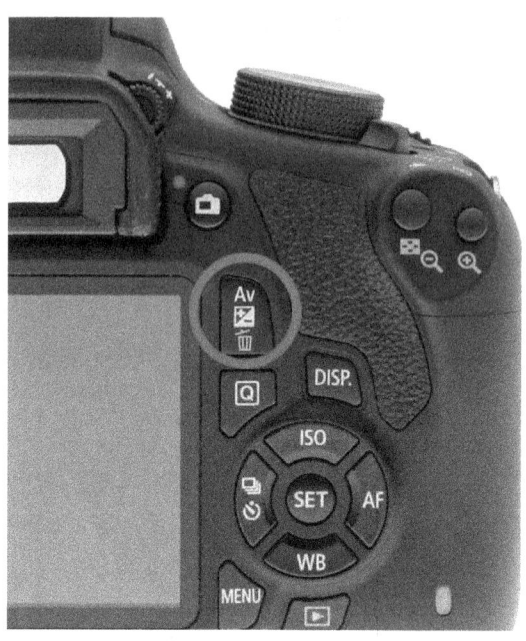

   b. Adjust Aperture with the dial

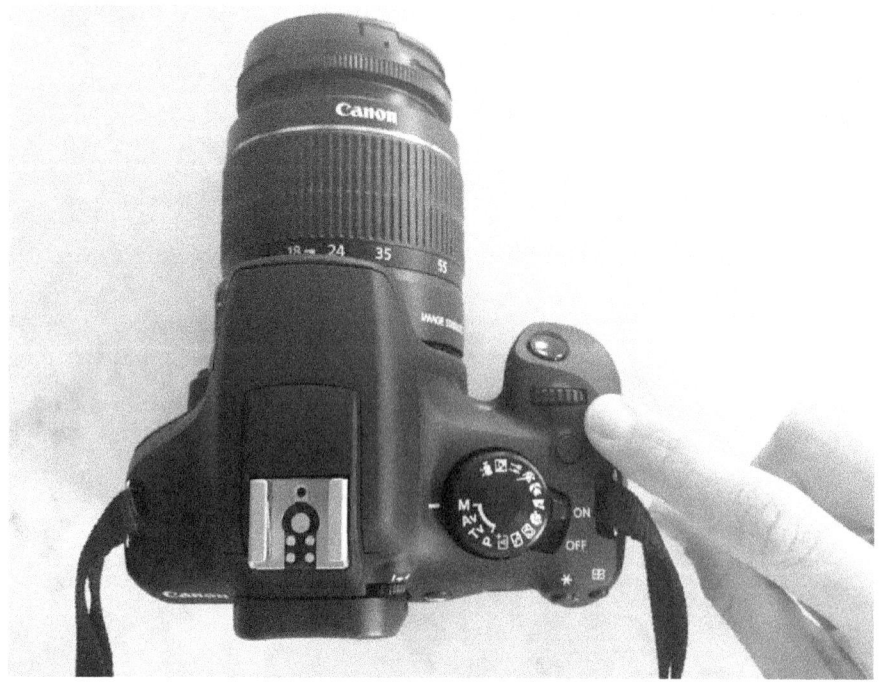

2. Adjusting Aperture in Nikon Camera
   a. Push +/- button

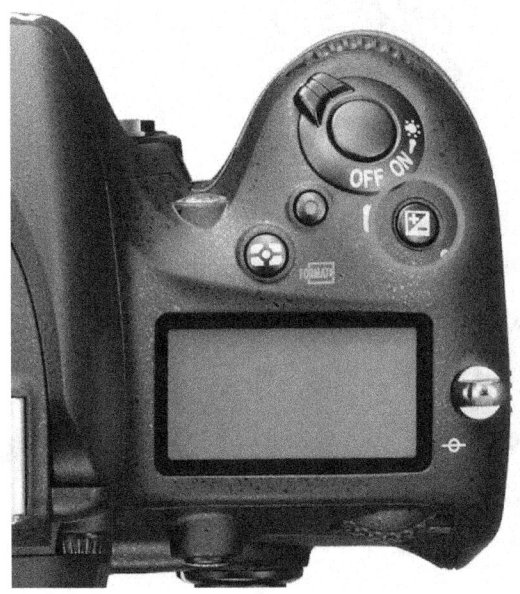

3. Adjust Aperture with the dial

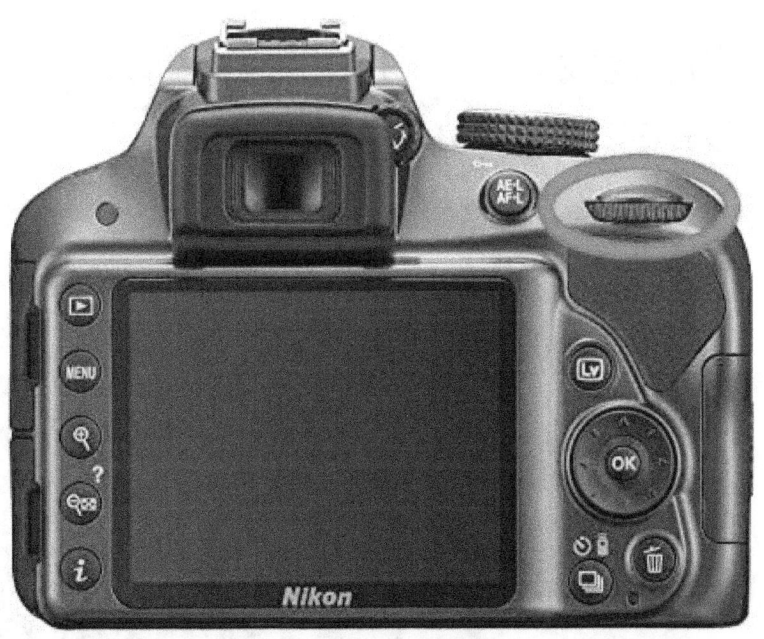

4. Adjusting Shutter Speed

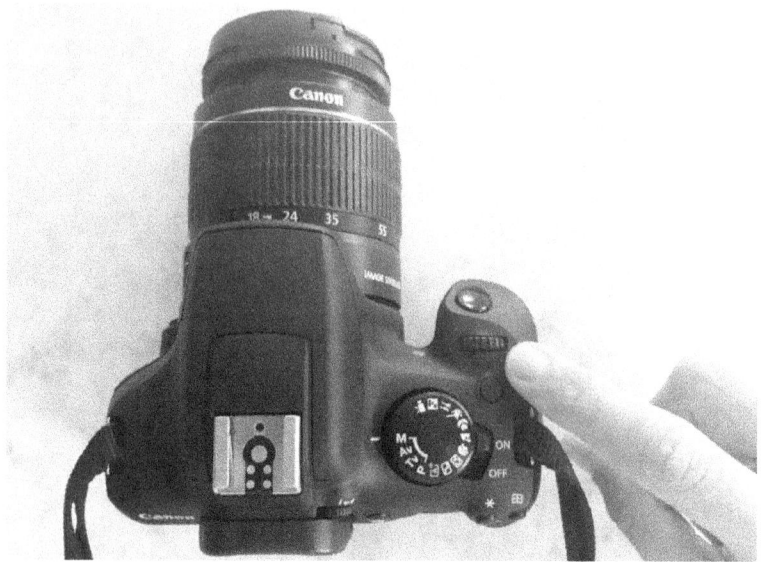

Just adjust the dial, it's the same for Canon and Nikon

5. Nikon camera Screen

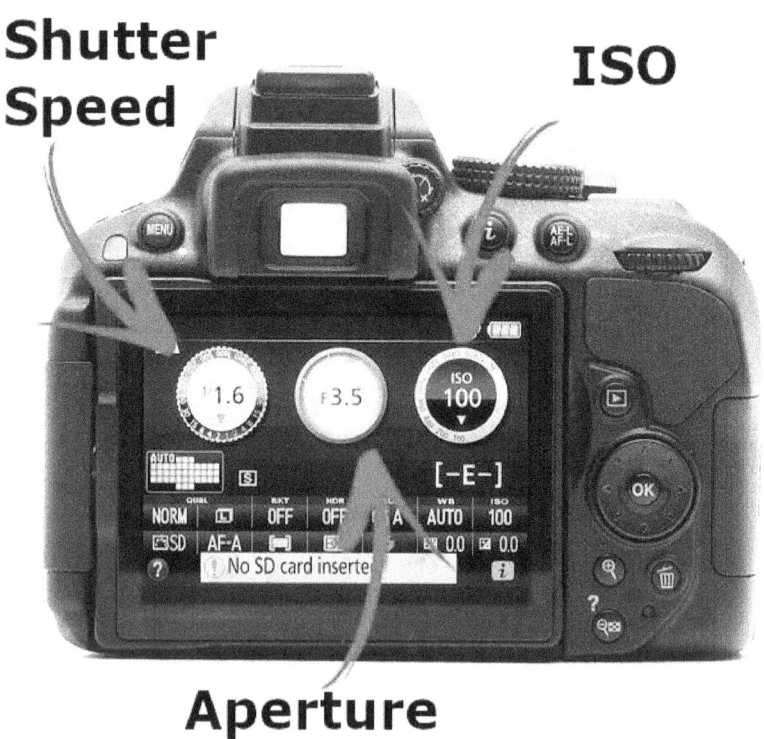

6. Canon camera Screen

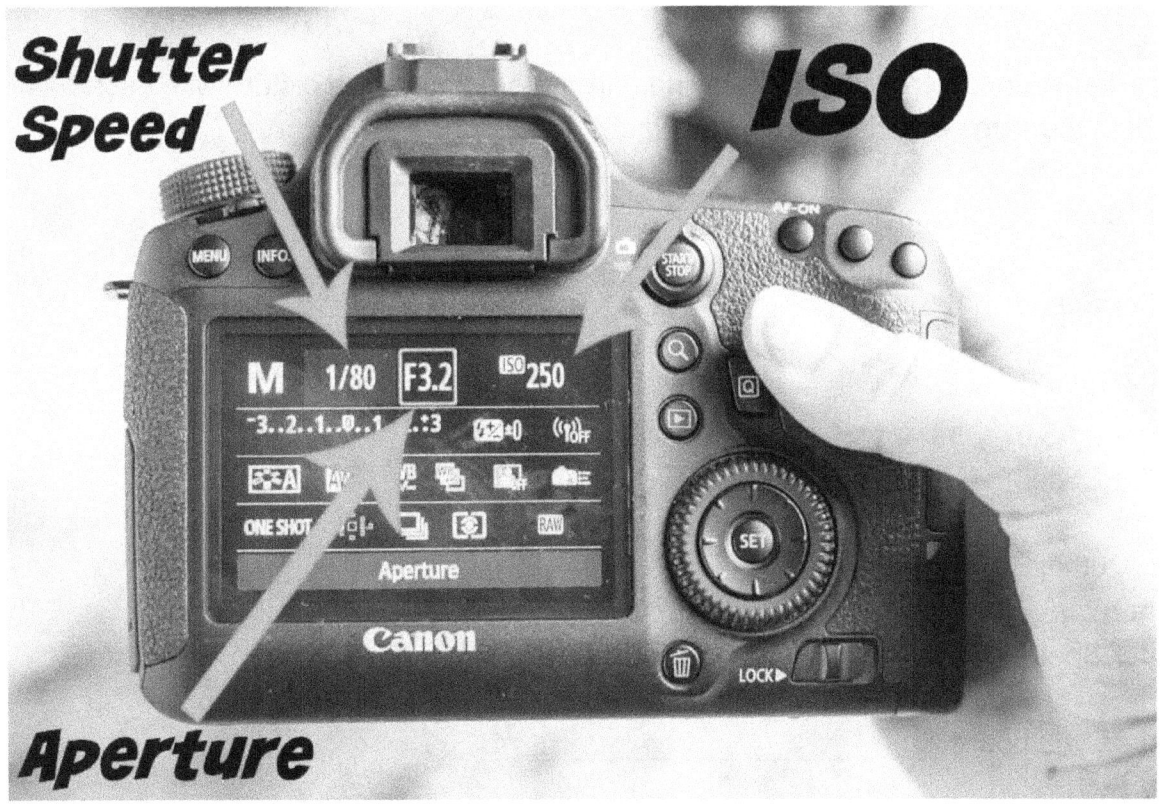

NOTE: All the practices are in Manual Mode (exceptions are specified).

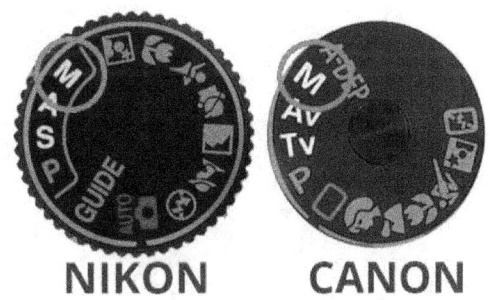

Practices

ISO

1. Set your camera with the following parameters and take a picture with each one to the same object outside in daylight:

ISO: 100
Aperture: f/5.6
Shutter Speed: 1/125

ISO: 1250
Aperture: f/5.6
Shutter Speed: 1/125

ISO: 3200
Aperture: f/5.6
Shutter Speed: 1/125

What do you notice:_____

Grain

2. Set your camera with the following parameters and take a picture with each one to the same object inside your house:

ISO: 100
Aperture: f/5.6
Shutter Speed: 1/125

ISO: 1250
Aperture: f/5.6
Shutter Speed: 1/125

ISO: 3200
Aperture: f/5.6
Shutter Speed: 1/125

Make zoom, what do you notice:_____

Aperture

3. Set your camera with the following parameters and take a picture with each one to the same object outside in daylight:

ISO: 400
Aperture: f/5.6
Shutter Speed: 1/250

ISO: 400
Aperture: f/11
Shutter Speed: 1/250

ISO: 400
Aperture: f/16
Shutter Speed: 1/250

What do you notice:

_____

4. Set your camera with the following parameters and take a picture with each one to the same object inside your house:

ISO: 400
Aperture: f/5.6
Shutter Speed: 1/250

ISO: 400
Aperture: f/11
Shutter Speed: 1/250

ISO: 400
Aperture: f/16
Shutter Speed: 1/250

What do you notice:

_____

Depth of field

5. This practice must be in Aperture Priority Mode:

   a. Set your camera in Aperture Priority Mode (A for Nikon, Av for Canon)

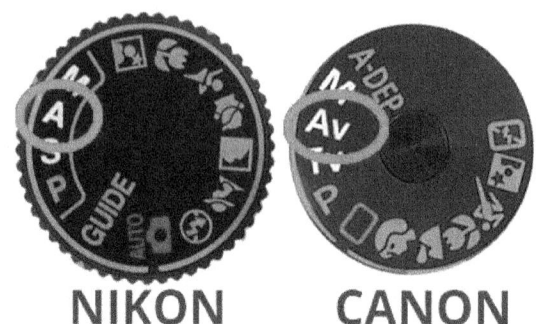

NOTE: This will automatically select Shutter speed for a correct exposure.

   b. Set your camera with the following parameters and take a picture with each one to the same object outside in daylight:

ISO: 400
Aperture: 1.8 (or the lowest your camera allows)

ISO: 400
Aperture: 3.5

ISO: 400
Aperture: 5.6

ISO: 400
Aperture: F8

ISO: 400
Aperture: F16

   Set an object in front of you (2 - 3ft), it can be any object, a toy, bottle, coffee mug, etc. and focus on this object, don't let the object cover the complete image, let some background to show. The background has to be far from the object.

What do you notice:
_____

6. This practice must be in Aperture Priority Mode:

    a. Set your camera in Aperture Priority Mode (A for Nikon, Av for Canon)

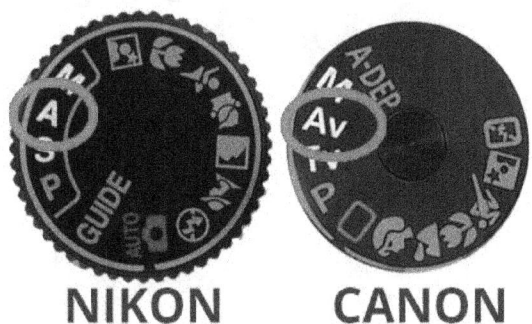

NOTE: This will automatically select Shutter speed for a correct exposure.

    b. Set ISO to 800
    c. Line up a couple of objects on a table in front of your camera. It can be toys, mugs, figures or any objects that are easy to focus upon (have lots of lines or contrast).
    d. During this practice your camera has to be still, so place it on the table. Place your first object directly in front of the camera, about 2 feet (0.6 meters) away. The second object at 1 foot (0.3 meters) beyond the first, and the third object another foot beyond the second. It should look something like this:

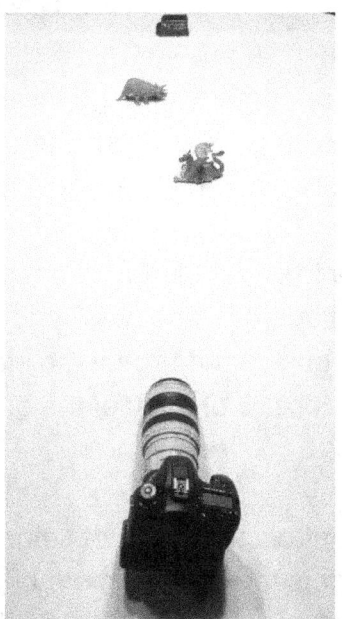

    e. The objects should be staggered sideways to ensure they are all visible from the camera angle.

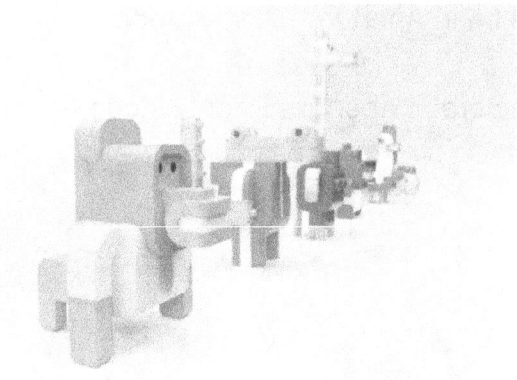

f. Direct your camera at the first object (so the active focus point is on it), and your camera focuses there.
g. Set your aperture to the smallest f-number your camera reaches; it will be around f/1.8 or f/3.5 and take a photograph.

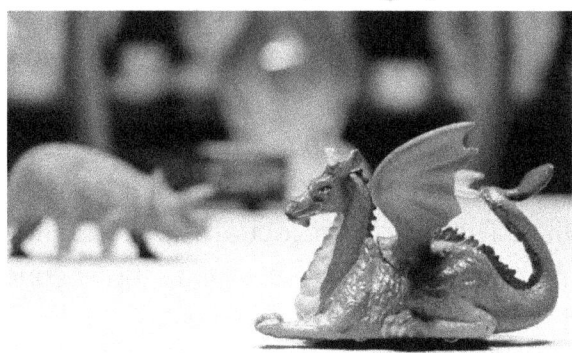

h. Without moving your camera, change the aperture to f/8 and take another photograph. Then change your aperture to the largest number your camera reaches; this might be f/22 or even higher and take a third photograph.
i. Move your camera to direct the focus point at the second object, repeat steps g and h. So you have another 3 photographs.
j. Focus on the third object and repeat the steps g and h. You should now have nine photographs; 3 of each of the objects in sharp focus, at three different apertures.

The aperture on your camera controls the depth of field. What do you notice as the aperture number (or f-number) gets larger? Are more or less things in focus? What about when you focus on an object further away and look at the same aperture setting as a close object? Is more or less in focus?

Shutter Speed

7. Set your camera with the following parameters and take a picture with each one to the same object outside in daylight:

ISO: 100
Aperture: f/5.6
Shutter Speed: 1/125

ISO: 100
Aperture: f/5.6
Shutter Speed: 1/1000

ISO: 100
Aperture: f/5.6
Shutter Speed: 1/4000

What do you notice:
_____

8. Set your camera with the following parameters and take a picture with each one to the same object inside your house:

ISO: 100
Aperture: f/5.6
Shutter Speed: 1/125

ISO: 100
Aperture: f/5.6
Shutter Speed: 1/1000

ISO: 100
Aperture: f/5.6
Shutter Speed: 1/4000

What do you notice:
_____

Movement
9. This practice must be in Shutter Speed Priority Mode:
    a. Set your camera in Shutter Speed Priority Mode (S for Nikon, Tv for Canon)

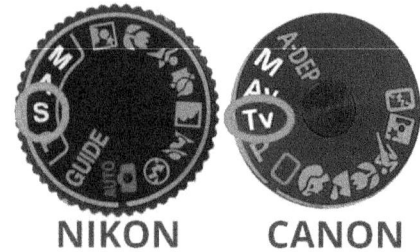

NIKON   CANON

NOTE: This will automatically select Aperture speed for a correct exposure.

    b. Go outside to a street with cars, zoom to the moving cars rims and take pictures with the following parameters in daylight:

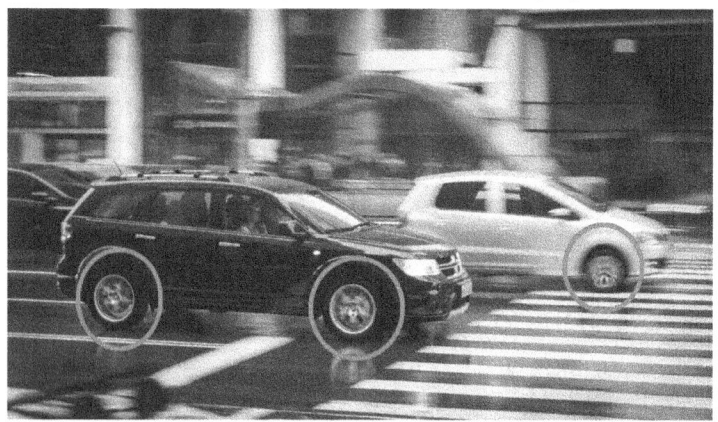

ISO: 400
Shutter Speed: 1/60

ISO: 400
Shutter Speed: 1/125

ISO: 400
Shutter Speed: 1/500

ISO: 400
Shutter Speed: 1/1000

ISO: 400
Shutter Speed: 1/4000

What do you notice:_____

10. Light Painting
    a. This practice needs complete darkness, so it's better to do it in the night or in a room with no windows.
    b. Set your camera in Manual Mode.
    c. 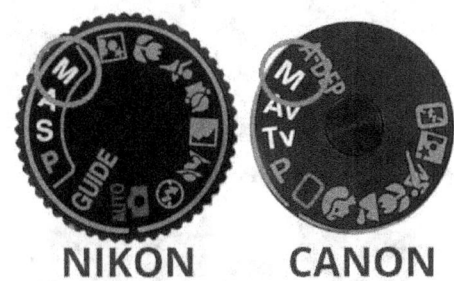 NIKON   CANON
    d. Set your camera with the following parameters:
        a. ISO: 100
        b. Aperture: F16
        c. Shutter Speed: 15"
    e. Set your focus to Manual. The camera has a hard time focusing in the dark, so usually manual focus works best.
    f. Set Self timer to 10"
    g. Use a tripod or place your camera still on a table.

Now the fun part Light Painting:

1. With the light of the room turned on, ask someone to stand up in front of the camera and do your best to focus your camera manually.
2. Get a light source ready (cell phone, flash light, flashing toy, etc.)
3. Press the shutter button to start taking the picture.
4. Turn off the light of the room.
5. Stand at the distance that you previously focused the camera.
6. Move the light source around.

    h. When the picture is finished see if 15 seconds was the right amount of time. If it's too dark and you need more light, adjust Shutter Speed to 20 or 30 seconds. If it was too much time (your pic was too bright) adjust Shutter Speed to 10 or 5 seconds.
    i. Experiment and have fun.

The result should look something like this.

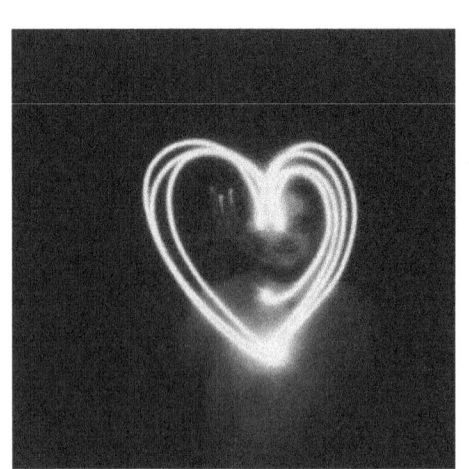
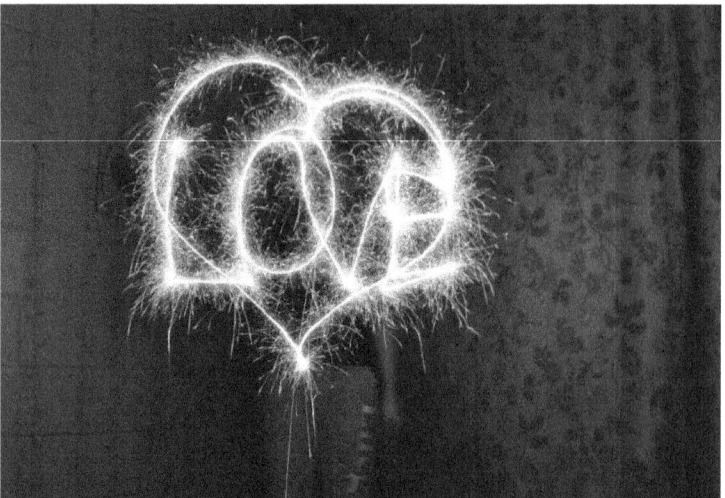
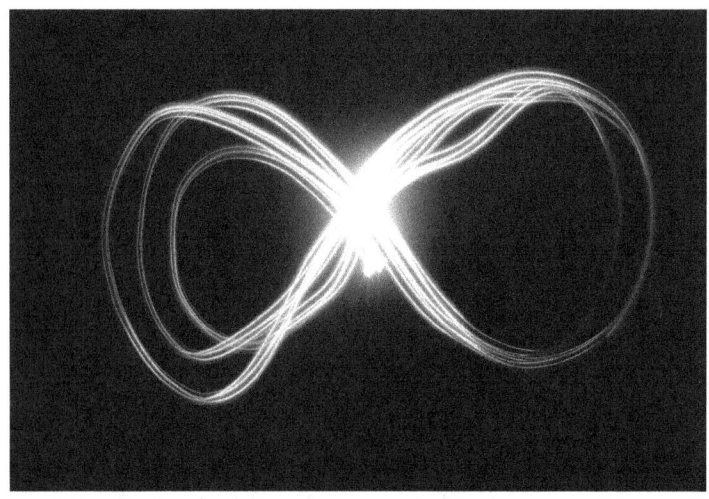
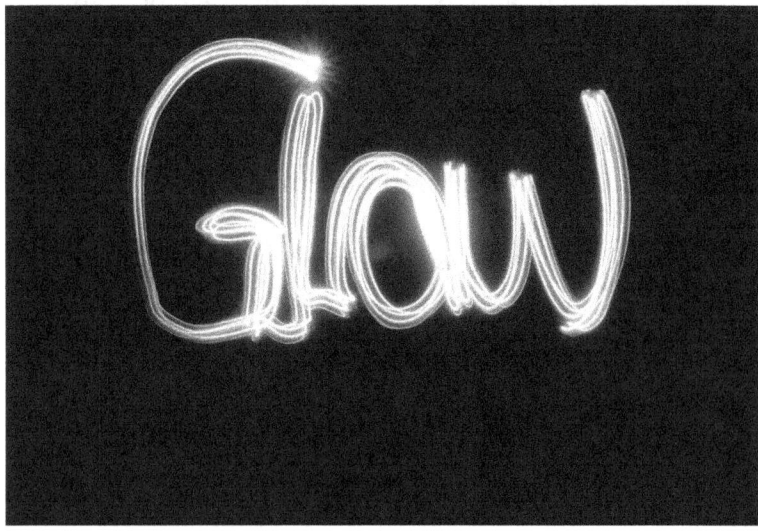

11. Go outside in a daylight and take a correctly exposed photo to an object that is directly in the sun with the following parameters:

ISO: Adjust
Aperture: Adjust
Shutter Speed: 1/4000

ISO: Adjust
Aperture: Adjust
Shutter Speed: 1/60

ISO: 6400
Aperture: Adjust
Shutter Speed: Adjust

ISO: 100
Aperture: Adjust
Shutter Speed: Adjust

ISO: Adjust
Aperture: f/3.5
Shutter Speed: Adjust

ISO: Adjust
Aperture: f/36
Shutter Speed: Adjust

Move to another place with shade and repeat the exercises.

NOTE: if your camera does not reach any parameter listed here, adjust to the lowest or highest your camera can reach.

12. Go outside in a daylight and take a correctly exposed photo to an object that is in a shadow with the following parameters:

ISO: Adjust
Aperture: Adjust
Shutter Speed: 1/4000

ISO: Adjust
Aperture: Adjust
Shutter Speed: 1/60

ISO: 6400
Aperture: Adjust
Shutter Speed: Adjust

ISO: 100
Aperture: Adjust
Shutter Speed: Adjust

ISO: Adjust
Aperture: f/3.5
Shutter Speed: Adjust

ISO: Adjust
Aperture: f/36
Shutter Speed: Adjust

Move to another place with shade and repeat the exercises.

NOTE: if your camera does not reach any parameter listed here, adjust to the lowest or highest your camera can reach.

13. Go outside in a sunset and take a correctly exposed photo to an object with the following parameters:

ISO: Adjust
Aperture: Adjust
Shutter Speed: 1/4000

ISO: Adjust
Aperture: Adjust
Shutter Speed: 1/60

ISO: 6400
Aperture: Adjust
Shutter Speed: Adjust

ISO: 100
Aperture: Adjust
Shutter Speed: Adjust

ISO: Adjust
Aperture: f/3.5
Shutter Speed: Adjust

ISO: Adjust
Aperture: f/36
Shutter Speed: Adjust

Move to another place with shade and repeat the exercises.

NOTE: if your camera does not reach any parameter listed here, adjust to the lowest or highest your camera can reach.

14. Go to the street and take pictures of moving objects (birds, dogs, people, bikes, cars, etc) with the following parameters in daylight:

    ISO: 100
    Aperture: adjust for correct exposure
    Shutter Speed: 1/60

    ISO: 400
    Aperture: adjust for correct exposure
    Shutter Speed: 1/1000

15. Outside in daylight set an object in front of you (2 - 3ft), it can be any object, a toy, bottle, coffee mug, etc. and focus on this object, don't let the object cover the complete image, let some background to show. The background has to be far from the object. Set your camera with the following parameters and take a picture to this object:

    ISO: 400
    Aperture: 3 or lower
    Shutter Speed: adjust

    ISO: 400
    Aperture: F5.6
    Shutter Speed: adjust

    ISO: 400
    Aperture: F16
    Shutter Speed: adjust

16. Restrictions: ISO

Go for a walk somewhere and leave all the walk ISO 400, adjust the other parameters for correct exposure, take a picture every 20 steps.

17. Restrictions: Aperture

Go for a walk somewhere and leave all the walk aperture f/5.6, adjust the other parameters for correct exposure, take a picture every 20 steps.

18. Restrictions: Shutter Speed

Go for a walk somewhere and leave all the walk aperture 1/250, adjust the other parameters for correct exposure, take a picture every 20 steps.

19. Freeze a water drop.

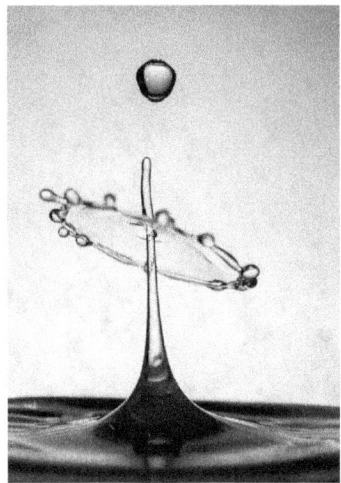

20. Grab a transparent recipient, fill it with water, drop something in it and freeze the splash.

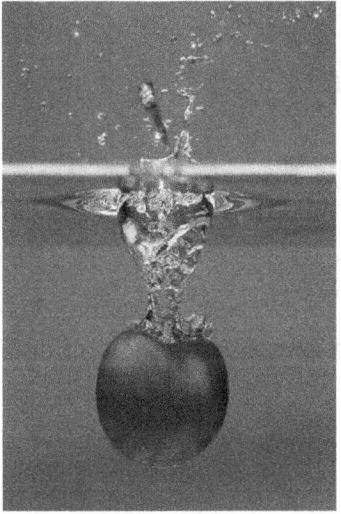

21. Play with the Depth of field. Place an object close to you (2-3 feet) and play with the aperture.

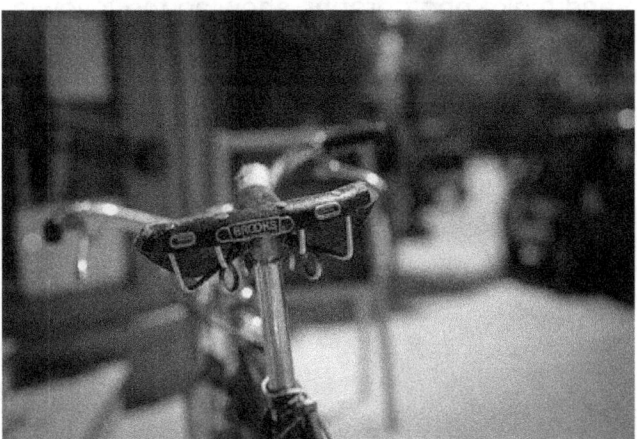

22. Fill balloons with water and freeze the explosion.

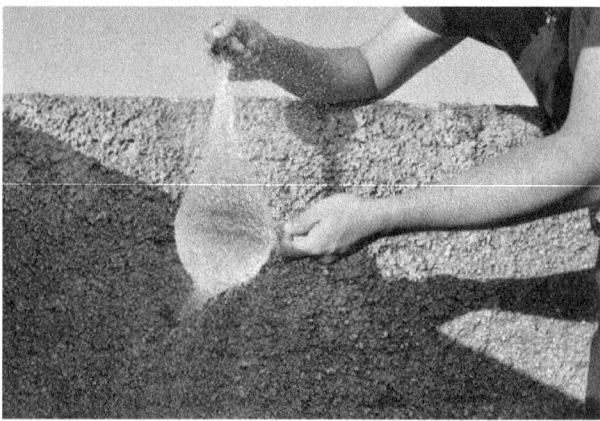

23. Go for a walk somewhere and show the movement.

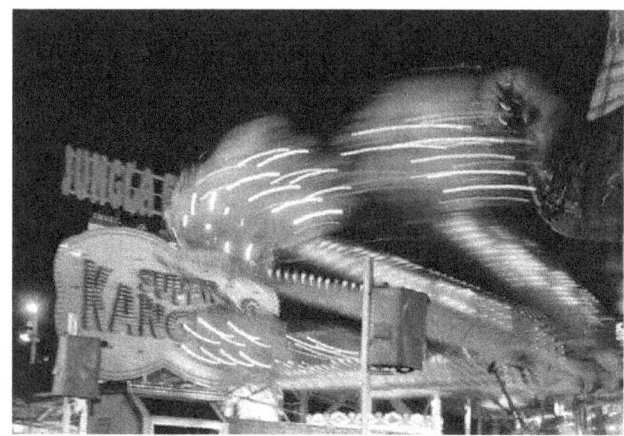

24. Go for a walk somewhere and Freeze fast objects.
25. A Dozen Photograph:

Pick a location. Stand in one spot and make 12 unique photographs while standing in the same place. You cannot move your feet.

26. Nine Elements:

Photograph these nine elements of a scene while in one location. Go to a street corner, park, or other location and make photographs showing the following:

Light
Shadow
Line
Shape
Form
Texture
Color
Size
Depth

27. Steps

Go for a walk somewhere you have always wanted to photograph. As you walk, stop and take a unique image after a predetermined number of steps. It can be any number of steps you want, 10 or 20.

28. Find something rotating (fan, ceiling fan, etc)

    a. Get a good exposure
    b. Make the rotating object still
    c. Blur the foreground and background around.
    d. Keep the shot sharp from the foreground to the background.
    e. Blur in front of and behind the object and show the propeller's movement.
    f. Capture the movement of the propeller.

29. Take a photo with a small depth of field.
30. Take a photo with a large depth of field.

Exercises

1. For each picture write small or large depth of field and match the f/stop that you think it was used to take it:

 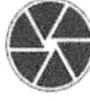 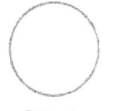 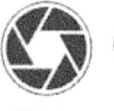  

f/4   f/16   f/1.4   f/5.6   f/2.8   f/8

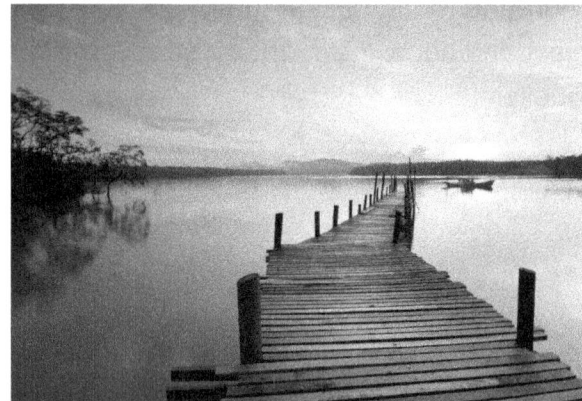 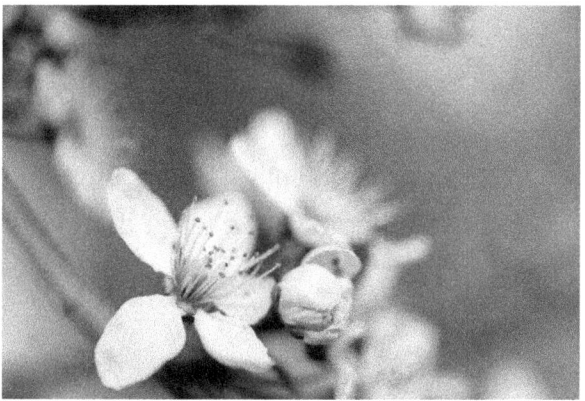

_____   _____

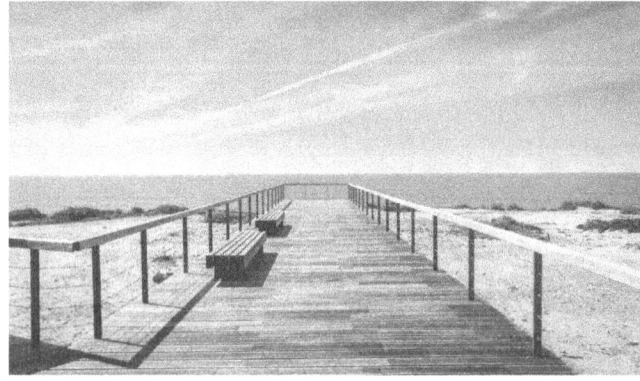 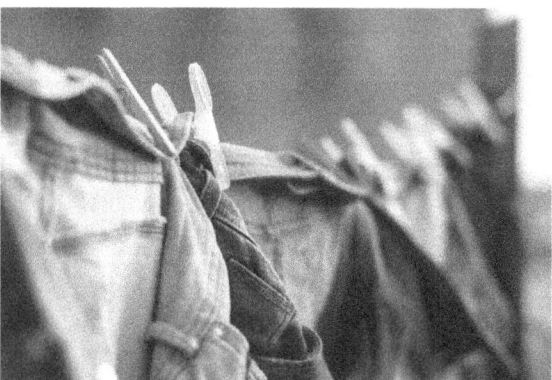

_____   _____

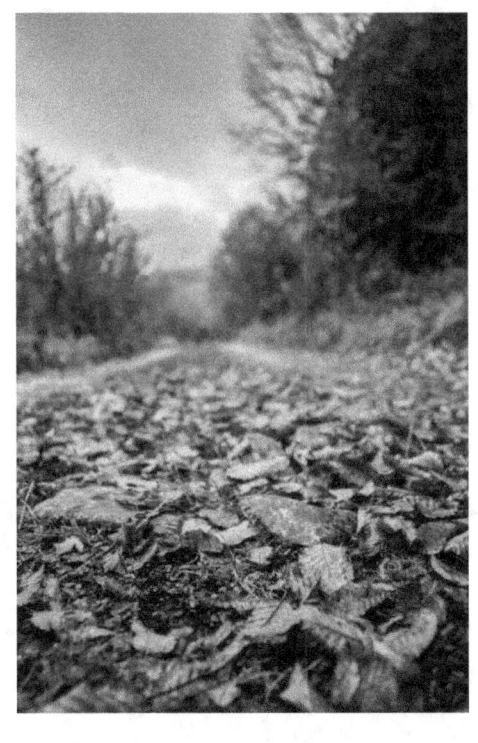
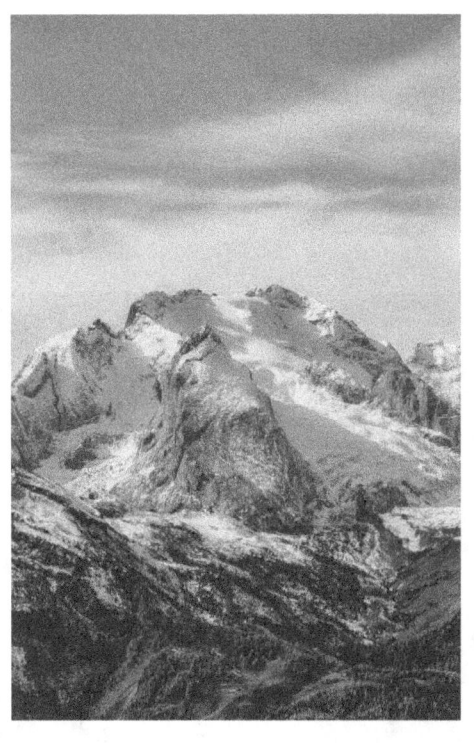
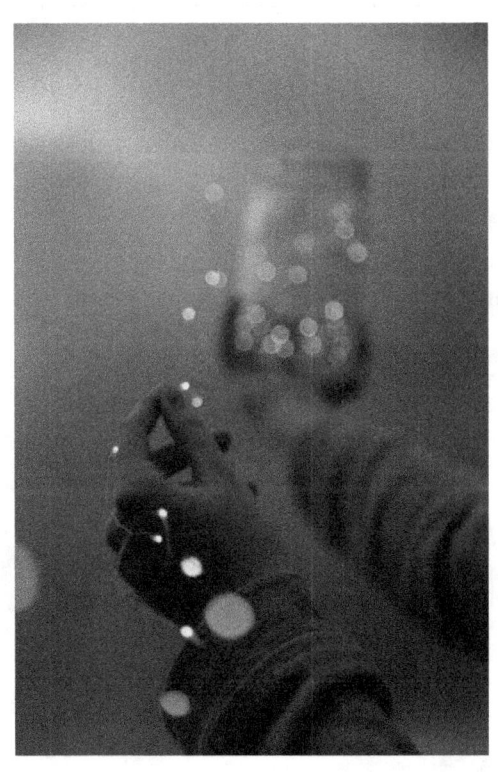
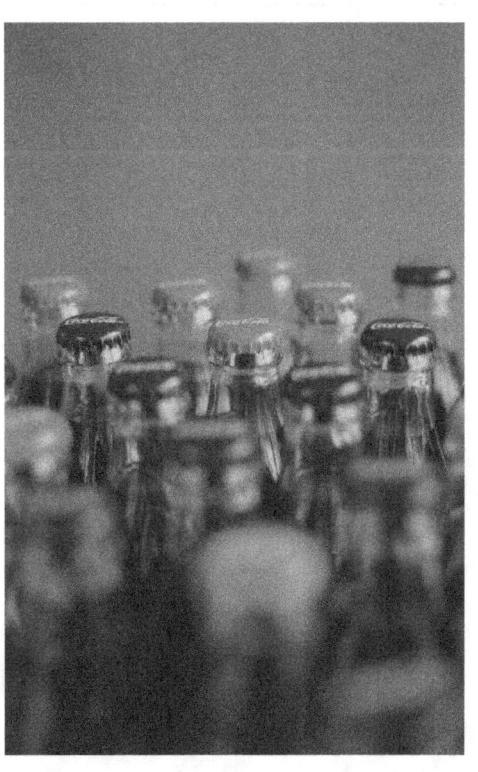

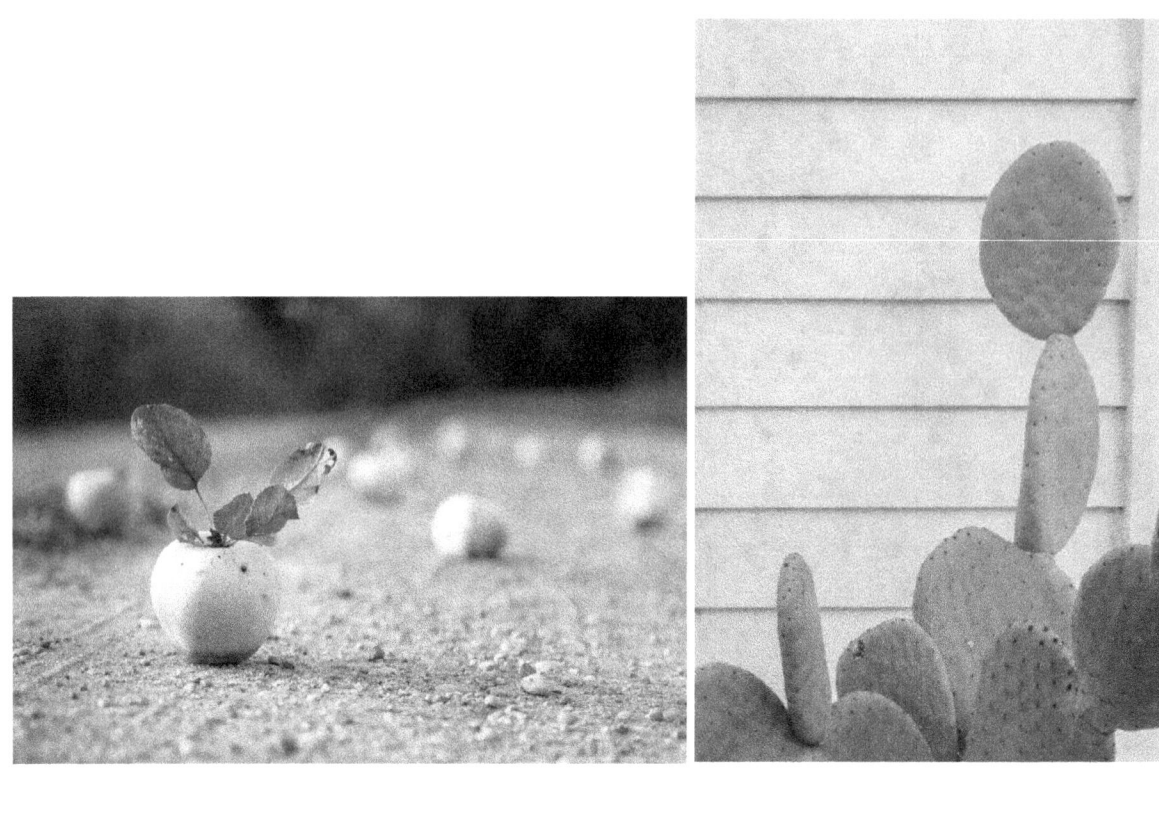

2. For each picture below decide which f/stop was used: f/22, f/5.6, f/3.5

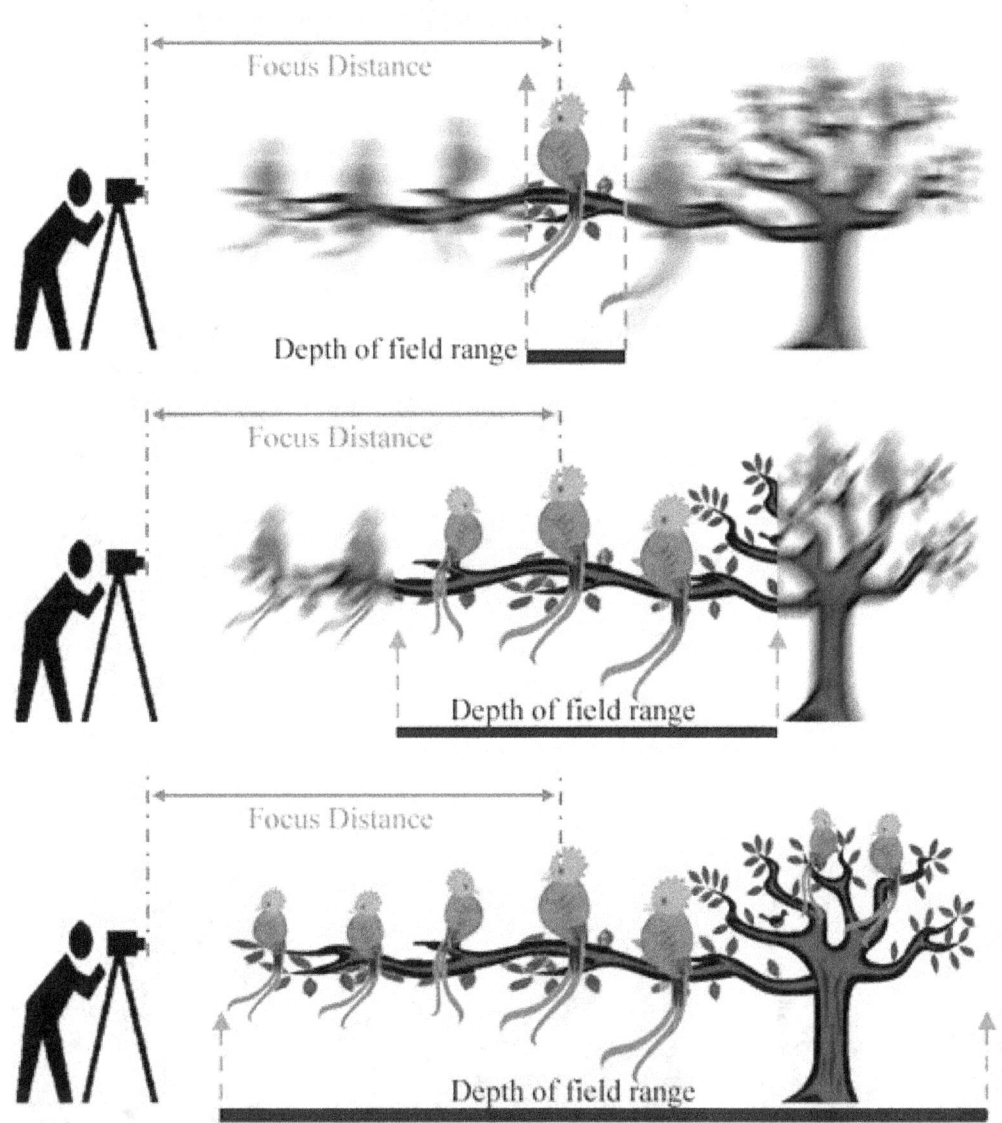

3. Match the photo to the aperture that was used to take it.

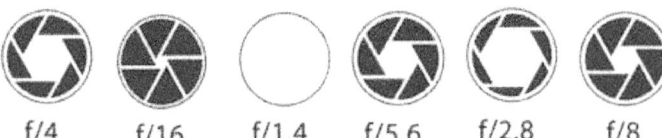

_____

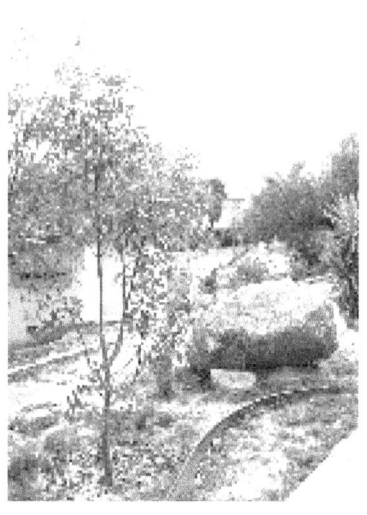
_____

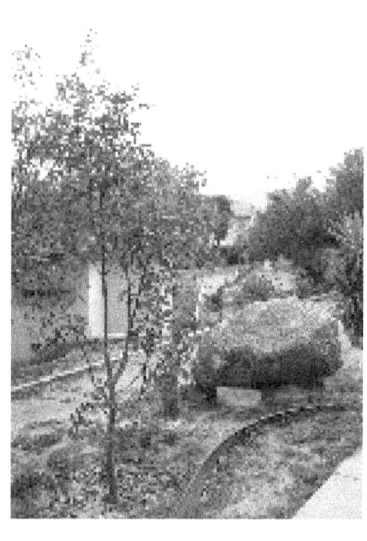
_____

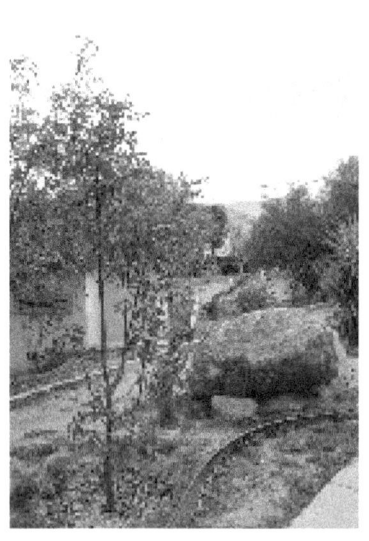
_____

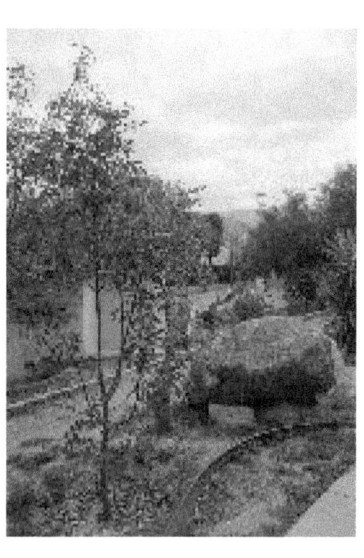
_____

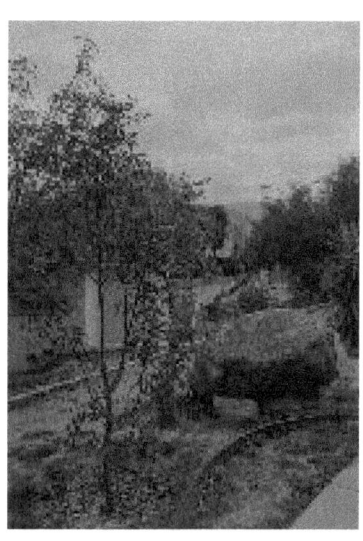
_____

4. Match the photo to the aperture that was used to take it.

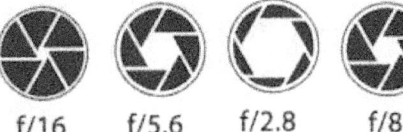

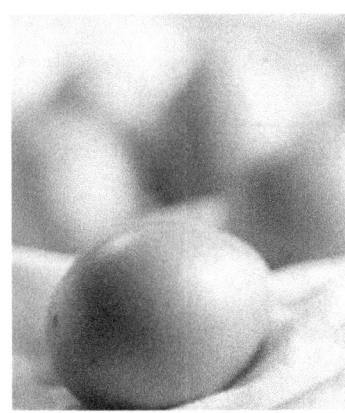

_____

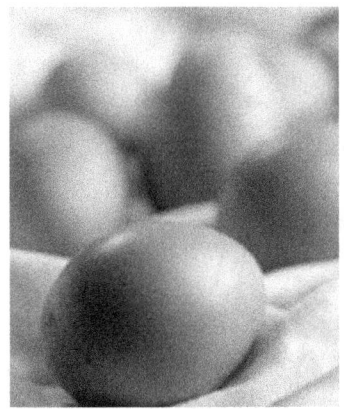

_____

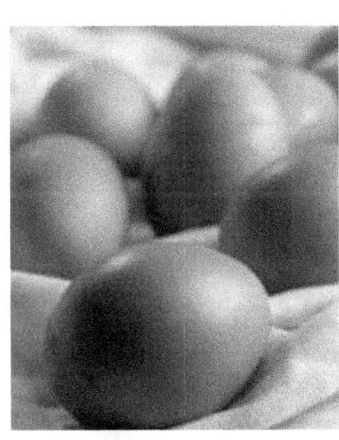

_____

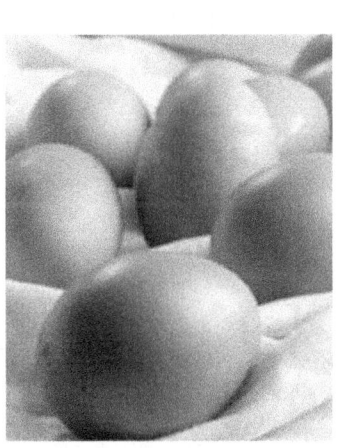

_____

5. Match the photo to the aperture that was used to take it.

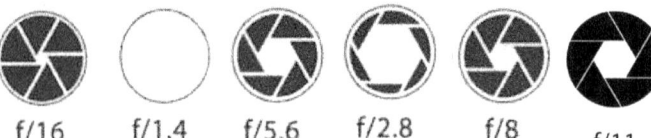

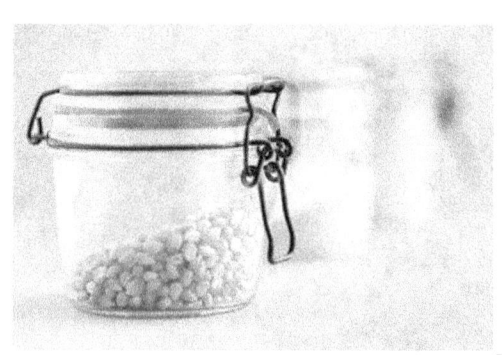 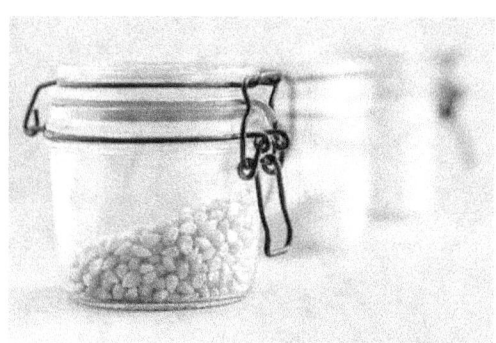

_____ _____

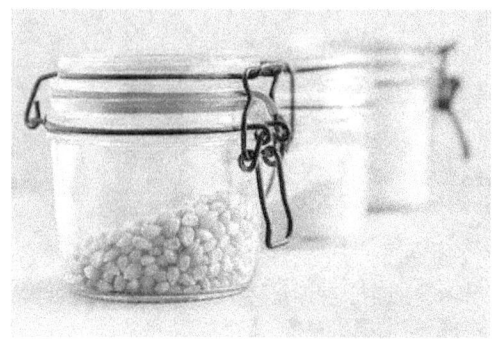 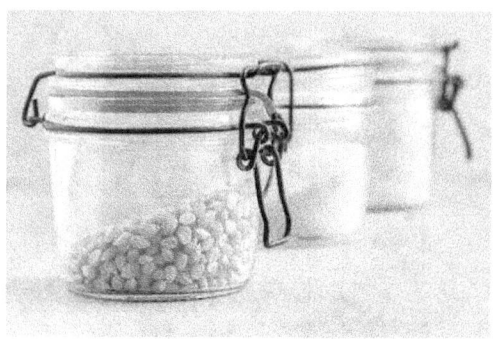

_____ _____

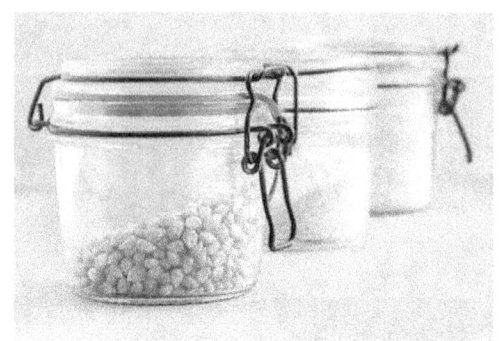 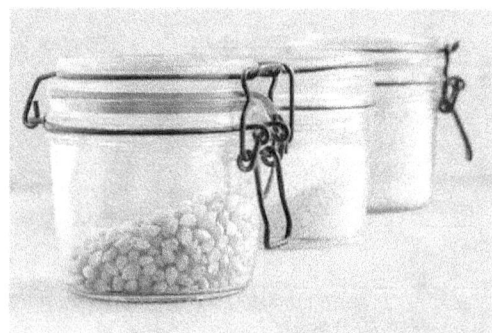

_____ _____

6. For each picture write fast or slow Shutter Speed:

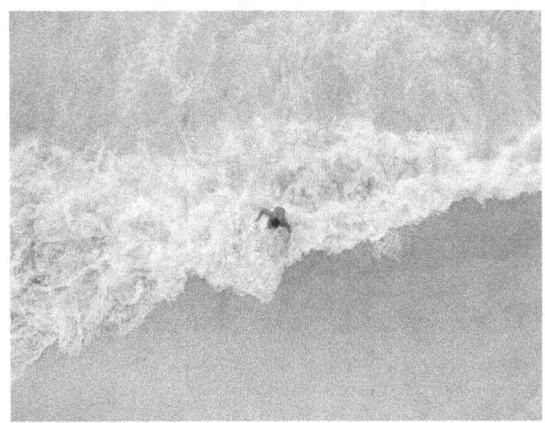

_____

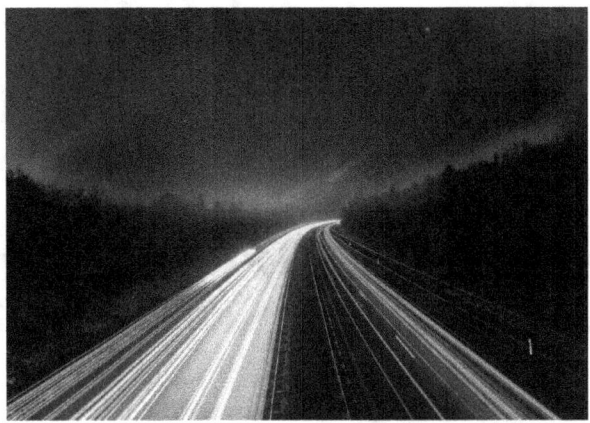

_____

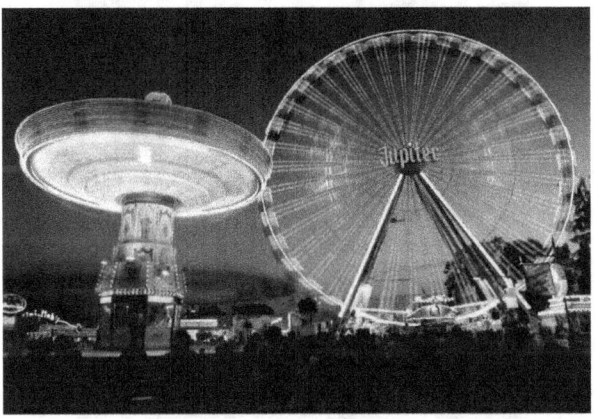

_____

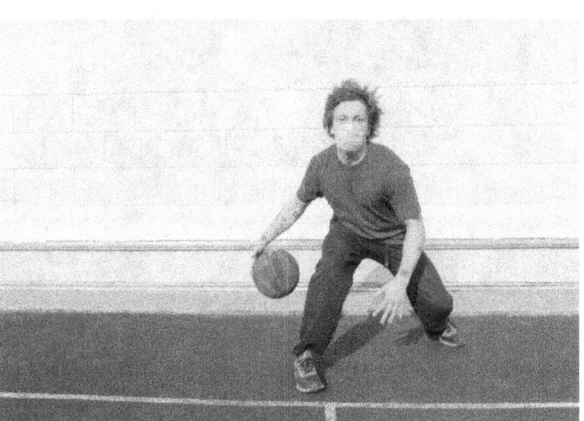

_____

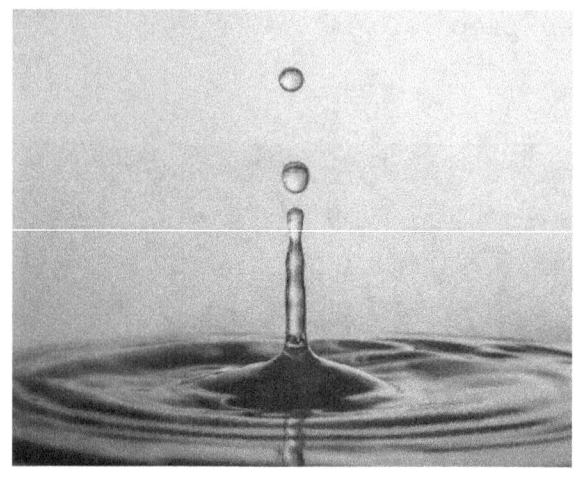

_____

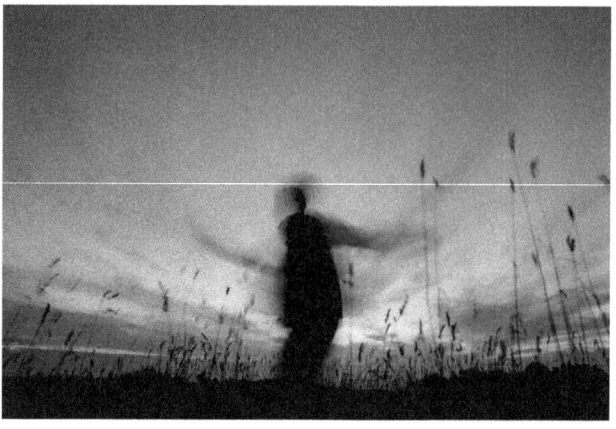

_____

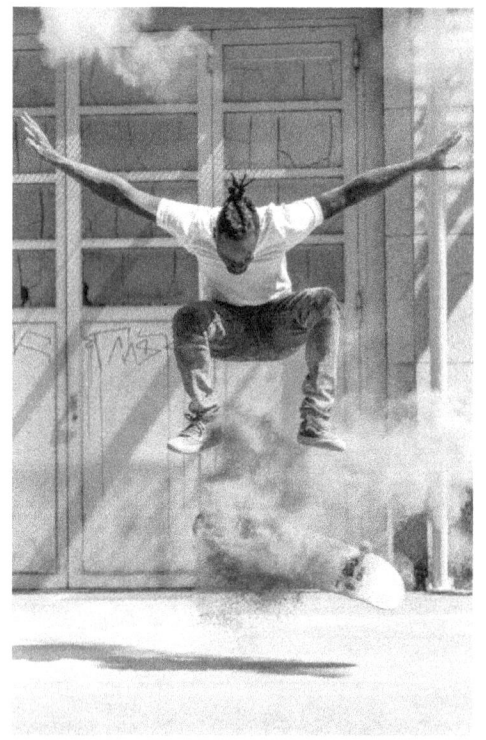

_____

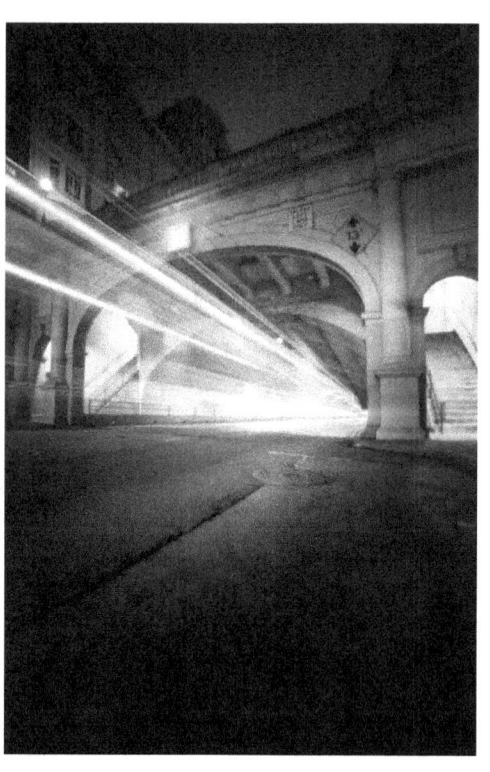

_____

Quiz

1. A camera's aperture controls the amount of light entering the camera by:
    a. Adjusting the size of the opening
    b. Opening and closing for a set amount of time
    c. Focusing on the background
    d. Changing the ISO setting

2. Depth of field is the _____.
    a. Motion shown in a photograph
    b. Size of the zone of sharp focus
    c. The part of the picture that is blurry

3. A wide open aperture will cause a picture to have a _____ depth of field.
    a. Large
    b. small

4. In portraits you usually want to draw attention to your subject by keeping the background out of focus. What f/stop would best help you do this.
    a. f/5
    b. f/29

5. In landscape photography you usually want everything in focus. What f/stop would best help you do this?
    a. f/2
    b. f/29

6. A wide open aperture will let in a lot of light.
    a. True
    b. False

7. What is the slowest shutter speed you would want to use if you're shooting by hand and want clear pictures.
    a. 1 sec
    b. 1/60 sec
    c. 1/2 sec
    d. f/29

8. Which of the statements and diagrams below is correct, TOP or BOTTOM?
    a. Top
    b. Bottom

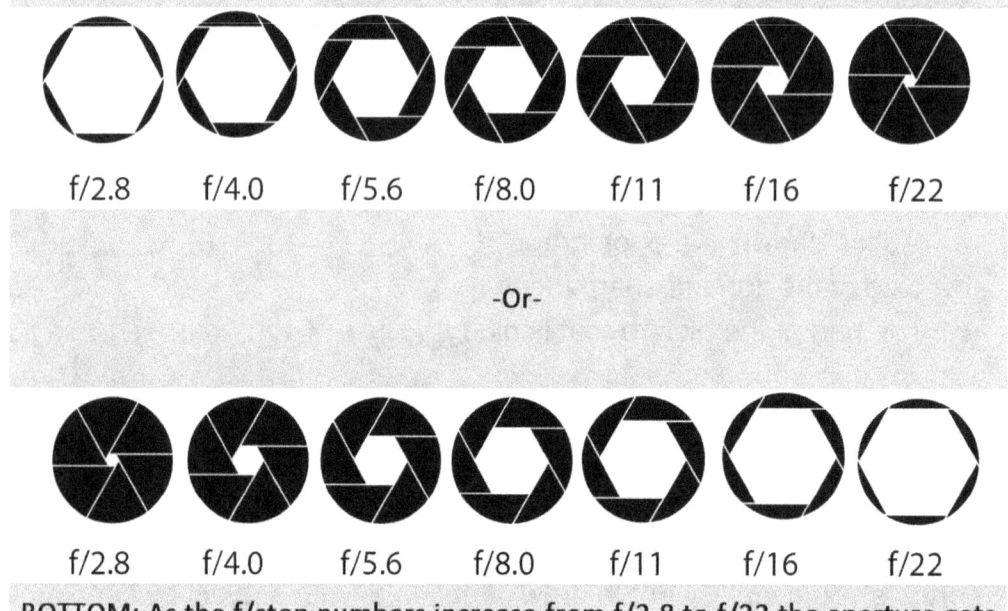

9. What type of depth of field does the photograph of the apples have?
    a. Large
    b. Small

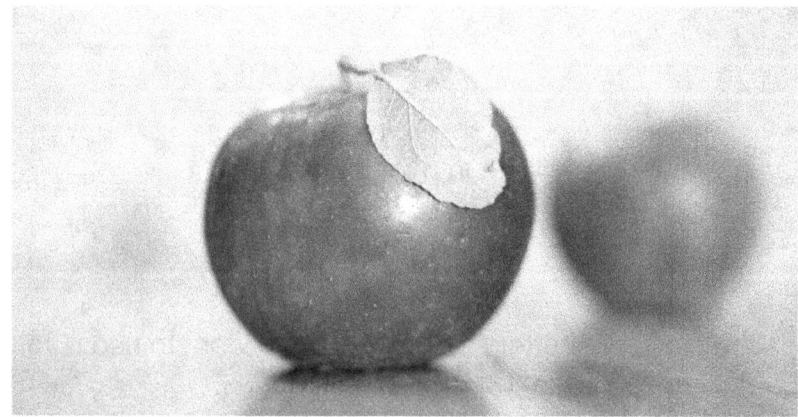

10. What f/stop was probably used to take the apple photograph?
    a. f/2
    b. f/32

11. What type of depth of field does the photograph of the city have? *
    a. Large
    b. Small

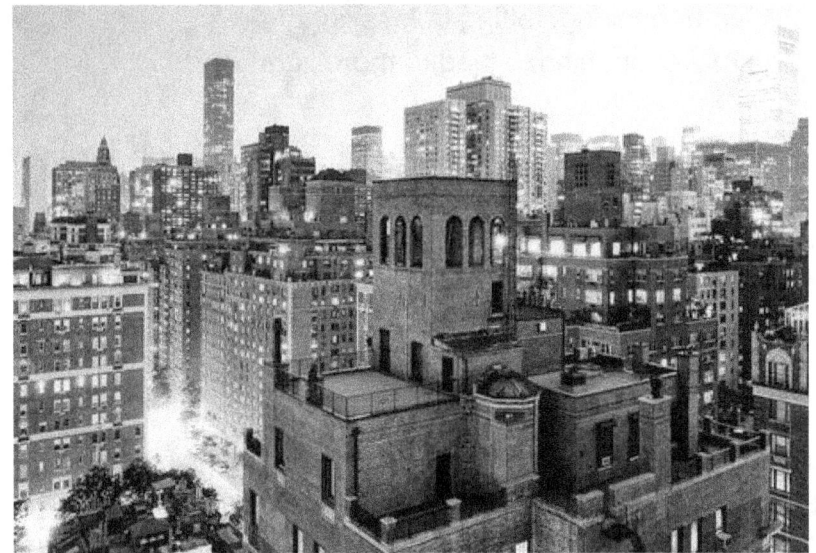

12. What f/stop was probably used to take the city photograph?
    a. f/3
    b. f/16

13. The camera's shutter speed controls the amount of light by adjusting the:
    a. Size of your lens opening
    b. Time light can enter the camera
    c. Sensitivity of the camera's sensor

14. Which kind of shutter speed tends to freeze motion?
    a. Fast
    b. Slow

15. Which kind of shutter speed lets in more light?
    a. Fast
    b. Slow

16. With a shutter speed of 1/4000, the camera lets in a large amount of light.
    a. TRUE
    b. FALSE

17. In aperture settings: compared to "f/8", the setting "f/16" is …
    a. a larger opening, letting in more light
    b. a smaller opening, letting in less light
    c. a larger opening, letting in less light
    d. a smaller opening, letting in more light

18. The _____ setting refers to the size of the gap that lets light get through the lens – similar to an eye's pupil.
    a. Exposure
    b. Aperture
    c. Shutter Speed
    d. telephoto lens

19. The shutter speed numbers range from single digits all the way up to 4,000 or more. This number is a measurement of the fraction of a _____ that the shutter is open.
    a. Second
    b. Minute
    c. Hour
    d. speed

20. The _____ is inside the lens and grows and shrinks to let in more or less light.
    a. Shutter
    b. Aperture
    c. ISO
    d. Pupil

21. To have certain things appear in focus and others to be blurred has to do with a measurement of ...
    a. Depth of field
    b. Shutter speed
    c. ISO
    d. Focus
    e. Metering mode

22. This is a measurement of traditional film, and measures your camera's sensitivity to light...
    a. ISO
    b. Aperture
    c. White Balance
    d. Color temperature

23. Which aperture would have the widest opening?
    a. f 2.8
    b. f 5.6
    c. f 11
    d. f 22

24. The three settings that make up the exposure triangle must stay _____ to give a good quality picture.
    a. the same
    b. Accurate
    c. Balanced
    d. In the composition

25. Once you get your settings balanced, you can keep the numbers there and use them for every situation.
    a. TRUE
    b. FALSE

26. A sports photographer that deals with motion is concerned with the _____ setting, which determines the amount of time the light is coming into the camera.
    a. Aperture
    b. Shutter Speed
    c. ISO

27. A high ISO number is _____ sensitive to light.
    a. Less
    b. More

28. If I set my f-stop to f1.8 and my shutter speed to 1/125th of a second and my ISO is maxed at 6400, yet my image is coming out dark. What can I do?
    a. Slow the shutter speed
    b. Open up the aperture
    c. Lower the ISO setting
    d. Change the white balance

29. With your ISO settings, you can adjust:
    a. How much light your lens is letting in at once (the size of the opening in the lens)
    b. How fast the shutter opens and closes
    c. How sensitive the camera is to light
    d. How your camera "sees" certain colors

30. The number 8" on the shutter setting means ...
    a. it will be open for 8 seconds
    b. it will be open for 8 minutes
    c. it will be open for 1/8 of a second
    d. it will be open for 1/8 of a minute

31. If I want to let in the LEAST amount of light, I would use which f-stop?
    a. f/2.8
    b. f/5
    c. f/8
    d. f/16

32. If I wanted the shallowest depth of field, I would use which of these apertures?
    a. f/1.4
    b. f/2.8
    c. f/8
    d. f/22

33. How can you control the exposure of a photo?
    a. Shutter Speed
    b. Aperture
    c. ISO
    d. Shutter speed, Aperture and ISO

34. Too much light creates an over bright image with lots of white, this is called what...

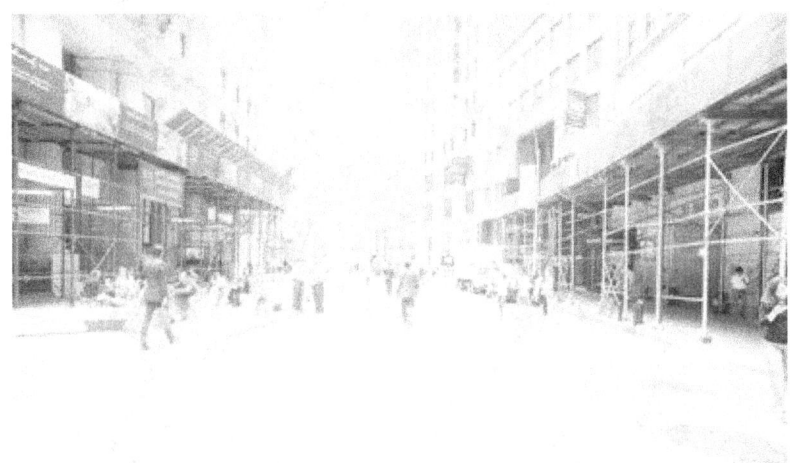

   a. Over exposed
   b. Under exposed

35. This photo shows what?

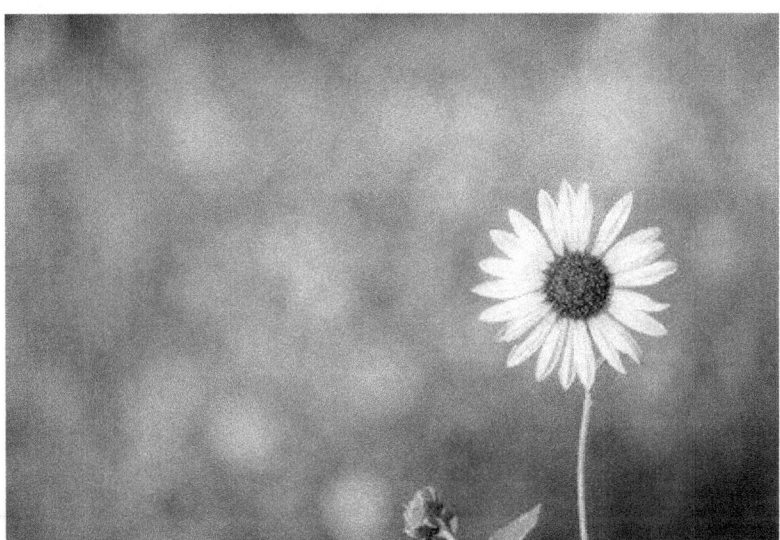

   a. Large (or deep) depth of field
   b. Small (or shallow) depth of field

36. This photo shows what?

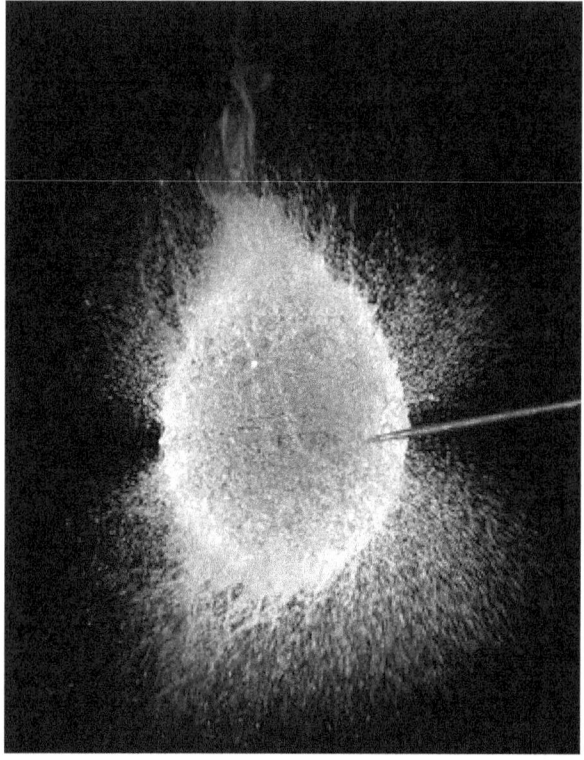

   a. Slow shutter speed
   b. Fast shutter speed

37. This photo shows what?

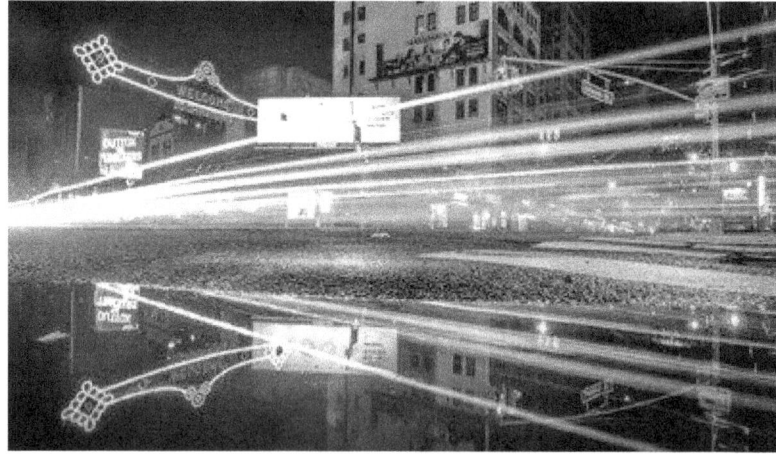

   a. Slow shutter speed
   b. Fast shutter speed

38. Using the camera in M (Manual mode) means you can control what?
    a. Shutter speed
    b. Aperture
    c. ISO
    d. Shutter speed, aperture and ISO

39. This image shows what?

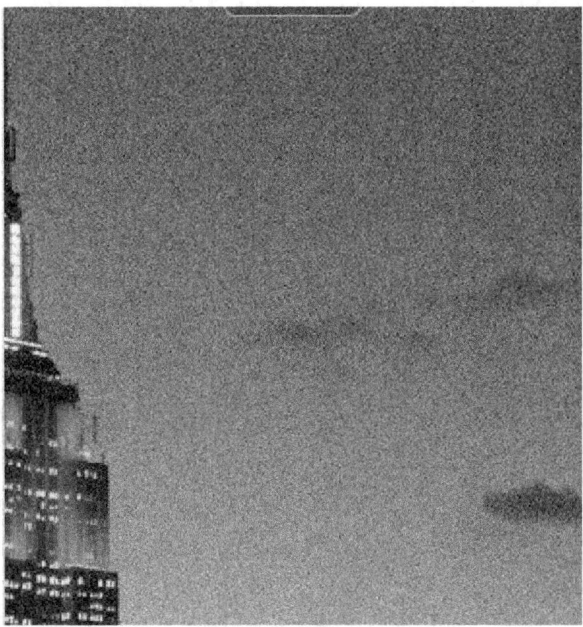

    a. Low ISO
    b. High ISO

40. 1/2500 is a .... shutter speed
    a. Slow
    b. Fast

41. The amount of time measured when light passes through the camera lens is defined by the:
    a. Aperture
    b. Shutter Speed
    c. ISO
    d. Exposure

Cheat Cheats
ISO

100   Full Sun, no shade

200   Lots of sun, could be in partial shade or an overcast day out in the open

200   Inside on a sunny day, directly by a large window

400   In the shade on a sunny day or under a covered area on an overcast day

700   Inside on a sunny or overcast day (near a window)

640-800   Sun is starting to set and less light

Noise Warning

800   Inside, quite a distance from a window (sunny outside)

850-1000   Inside, quite a distance from a window (overcast day)

1250   Inside during the evening, light bulbs are the only source of light

1600   Inside a dark room where there is a light source (theatre, school production, etc)

Aperture

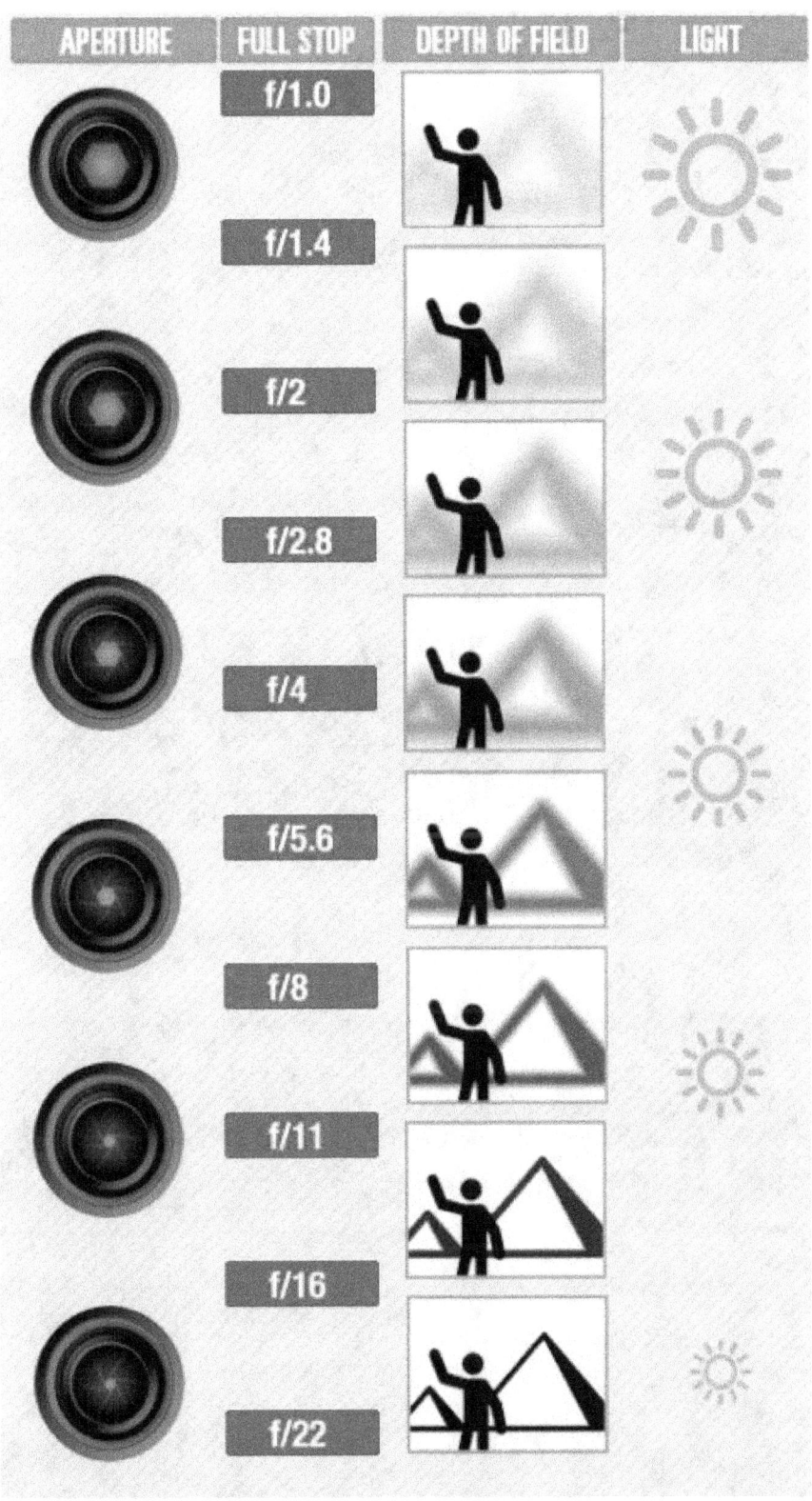

Shutter Speed

1/4000	🕐	Freezing very fast subject
1/2000	🚗	Freezing cars/birds
1/1000		Freezing cars
1/500	⛳	Slow sports
1/250	👧👦	Kids
1/60	📷	Slow hand movement
1/15		Blur moving cars/fast subjects
1/8	〰️	Blur fast moving water
1/2	〰️	Blur slow moving water
1 sec +	💧	Blur water (smooth water effect)

EXPOSURE

UNDER EXPOSED   **PERFECT** According to the camera   **OVER EXPOSED**

APERTURE

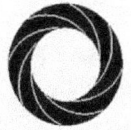 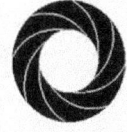 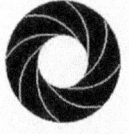  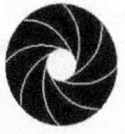 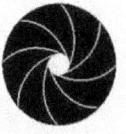 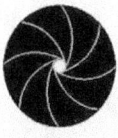

f/1.8   f/2.8   f/4   f/5.6   f/8   f/11   f/16   f/22

SHALLOW DEPTH OF FIELD   DEEP DEPTH OF FIELD
LESS IN FOCUS   MORE IN FOCUS
BLURRY BACKGROUND   SHARPER BACKGROUND

SHUTTER SPEED

BULB   30"   15"   10"   2"   1"   1/25   1/30   1/50   1/100   1/125   1/250   1/320   1/500   1/1000   1/2000

LONGER EXPOSURE   SHORTER EXPOSURE
BLURRY SHOTS   SHARPER SHOTS
MORE LIGHT   LESS LIGHT

RULE OF THIRDS

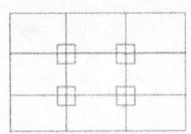   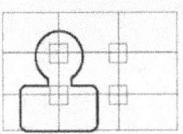   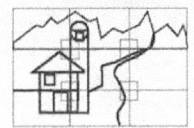   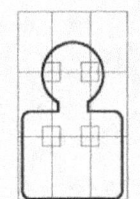

Rule of Thirds   Landscape position   Landscape position   Portrait position

ISO

100   250   320   400   500   640   800   1000   1250   1600   2000   2500   3200

LOW SENSITIVITY TO LIGHT   HIGH SENSITIVITY TO LIGHT
FOR USE DURING DAY LIGHT OR TO HELP REDUCE NOISE   FOR USE DURING NIGHT OR LOW LIGHT
LESS NOISE   CREATES EXTRA NOISE

www.ingramcontent.com/pod-product-compliance
Lightning Source LLC
Chambersburg PA
CBHW080520220526
45465CB00006B/2545